Mahatma Gandhi on Untouchability

Also Available:

- — Mahatama Gandhi on Ethics
- — Mahatma Gandhi on Sarvodaya
- — Revisiting Hind Swaraj
- — Mahatma Gandhi on Untouchability
- — Understanding Gandhi

About the Author

Anil Dutta Mishra is a distinguished Gandhian scholar and writer. He started his career as Assistant Professor in the Department of Non-violence and Peace Studies, Jain Vishva Bharati University, Ladnun, Rajasthan, became Deputy Director of National Gandhi Museum and Honorary Professor, Centre for Gandhian Philosophy and Human Development, Gayatri Vidya Parishad Degree College (Autonomous), Visakhapatnam.

Dr Mishra has held the post of General Secretary of Indian Society of Gandhian Studies, Alliance for Sarvodaya, Member Board of Studies, Nagpur and Punjab Universities and is Member of Gandhian Studies Centre of different colleges and universities across India sponsored by UGC and Executive Member IIPA Regional Branch. He has authored/edited 30 books and published a number of research papers. His recent book *Reading Gandhi* is widely acclaimed.

Email: anilduttamishra@gmail.com

MAHATMA GANDHI ON UNTOUCHABILITY

Anil Dutta Mishra

CONCEPT PUBLISHING COMPANY PVT. LTD.
NEW DELHI-110059

ISBN-13 : 978-93-5125-121-7

First Published 2015

Published and Printed by

Concept Publishing Company Pvt. Ltd.
A/15-16, Commercial Block, Mohan Garden
New Delhi-110059 (India)
T: 25351460, 25351794, *F*: 091-11-25357109
E: publishing@conceptpub.com, W: www.conceptpub.com
Editorial Office: H-13, Bali Nagar, New Delhi-110 015, India.

Cataloging in Publication Data--*Courtesy:* D.K. Agencies (P) Ltd. <docinfo@dkagencies.com>

Mishra, Anil Dutta, 1965-
Mahatma Gandhi on untouchability / Anil Dutta Mishra.
p. cm.
Includes bibliographical references and index.
ISBN 9789351251217

1. Gandhi, Mahatma, 1869-1948—Political and social views. 2. Dalits—India. I. Title.

DDC 305.56880954 23

Preface

Untouchability is a greatest sin and crime against individual and society. Gandhi from early childhood relentlessly worked against untouchability. In fact he has been opposed to untouchability since the age of twelve, when his mother scolded him for brushing shoulders with a young *Bhangi* named Uka and insisted to undergo purification. In Indian society purification was at that time a common ritual. In the purification process one should take bath and wash all the clothes which he or she was wearing at that time or sprinkle *Ganga Jal* on the body if he/she is not in a position to take bath. Gandhi had a deep understanding of Indian history, civilization, culture and society. So, he was doing something completely original for the removal of untouchability without creating any disharmony in the indivudual and society. He looked at and understood untouchability from an angle no one was able to. His vision and method was direct, and this directness was, and is, revolutionary. He was fighting for the removal of untouchability and at the same time empowering the powerless, voiceless, poverty ridden deprived section of the Indian society. His means may be different but his aim was to remove the untouchability from the society. One can understand that in Indian context law alone is not enough rather you have to change the mindset of the individual and society. And Gandhi was doing that.

Mahatma Gandhi's statement on Untouchability will be an eye-opener for the general readers and critics to understand his crystal clear view on untouchability. These writings show how much Gandhi was concerned for the upliftment of untouchables and end of untouchability . Gandhi's writings are reproduced here without any distortion and alteration so that the readers draw their own conclusions. To make the book reader friendly it has been divided into two parts. In part one, an attempt has been made to introduce the subject keeping all the contemporary discourses and challenges in mind. In part two, Gandhi's original writings entitled 'Statement of Untouchability' is placed for reader's deeper understanding of the subject.

I am sure that the book 'Mahatma Gandhi on Untouhability' will open new vistas of research and proper understanding of Gandhi on this issue.

In writing this book I had received, over the years, very valuable help from friends, teachers and colleagues. I am grateful to them. My family has always stood behind me in all my academic endeavours. My wife, Dr. Sweta Mishra, Associate Professor, Department of Political Science, Gargi College, University of Delhi, went through the final draft and provided her valuable inputs .

Last but not the least, I am grateful to Shri Ashok Kumar Mittal of Concept Publishing Company Pvt. Ltd., for bringing out this book in present form and that too within record time.

Anil Dutta Mishra
anilduttamishra@gmail.com

Contents

PART ONE
INTRODUCTION

1

Introduction

Gandhi was the first and pioneer leader who makes the removal of untouchability a life mission. Gandhi made untouchability a national issue. Gandhi fought for the removal of untouchability a blot on Indian humanity. His fight was unique and unparallel. He stressed, in the main, that the conscience of the so-called 'higher' castes in Hindu society had to be roused against the crime or the practice of untouchability, which has tarnished their image. Gandhi desired to deliver the untouchables, whom he called *Harijans*, from the slavery of centuries by means of changing the hearts of the Caste Hindus. This desire was as strong as his desire for freedom/ independence was. He had said that freedom would be meaningless if untouchability was not removed. He also said that attainment of *Swaraj* was a must, but that would not be complete unless a social order based on equality and fraternity was established. Gandhi through non-violence action wanted to remove the untouchability from root. In attacking untouchability Gandhi had gone to the very root of the matter and, therefore, it was an issue of transcendental value, far surpassing *Swaraj* in terms of political Constitutions and he said such a Constitution would be a dead-weight if it was not backed by a moral basis in the shape of the present hope engendered in the hearts of the down-trodden millions that the weight is going to be lifted from their shoulders.

Gandhi and Untouchability

Gandhi's ultimate search was for righteous conduct. For Gandhi, the means were more important than the end, and he believed that with the right means, desired ends were bound to follow. Gandhi showed India as well as the World the path of truth and non-violence. He believed that it was truth alone that prevailed in the end. According to him, India's real emancipation depended on the abolition of untouchability. He worked hard for the upliftment of the *Harijans*, the name given by him to the untouchables. Besides, Gandhi regarded untouchability a sin against God and Man.

Gandhi's influence over the masses was tremendous. The people of India had unflinching faith in him. The most remarkable feature of his leadership was that he was able to lead and direct the movement without holding any position of power of any high office. He was able to command the respectful obedience of millions though there was nothing divine about Gandhi. However, he was also accepted as a great emancipated saviour and Messiah for the socially downtrodden and the victims of socio-economic exploitation. Gandhi had spoken and written more on untouchability than any other leader in India. He had publicly put abolition of untouchability as the essential prerequisite for India's independence.

Varna-ashram and *Purusharthas* are both unique feature of Indian social order. At the same time, untouchability is the worst feature of the degraded caste system which is so deeply embedded in the minds of the Indian society that our entire outlook on life and politics is coloured by it. Caste is a reality and it peeped into every aspect of human activities in Indian society. It has erected a powerful barrier against the emotional integration of the people of India. It has divided them into high-born and low-born caste compartments. The degraded caste system have always exercised a predominant hold on the public and social life of Indian society. Untouchability has also remained a social concern for all those who have occupied any significant space in the Indian public domain.

Gandhi always held the high Caste Hindus responsible for the plight of the untouchables and he also asserted that the Hindus would have no right to claim *Swaraj*, as long as freedom, was not restored to the exploited classes. He believed that the political bondage of Indians was a well-deserved punishment meted out to them for observing untouchability. Therefore, at times, it is alleged what Gandhi categorically proclaimed that his *Harijan Seva* (upliftment) movement was not intended for upliftment of *Harijans*, but for the salvation of high caste Hindus as penance for the crime they had perpetrated against the *Harijans.*[1]

Gandhi aroused the people's attention more widely than anyone had done before in history, to the evils of untouchability. Gandhi took it upon himself to awaken the conscience of the human race. He sought to fight against the horrors of untouchability and the other social wrongs, which he found humiliating and shameful for Indian society. In 1925, Gandhi wrote, "untouchability is our greatest shame; the humiliation of it is sinking deeper".

In 1931, Gandhi named untouchable, the Shudras, and *Chandalas* as '*Harijan*' i.e. man of god. Gandhi wrote; "the 'untouchable: to me, is, compared to us, really a Harijan (a man of God), and we are *Durjan* (men of evil). For while the untouchable has toiled and moiled and dirties his hands so that we may live in comfort and cleanliness, we have delighted in suppressing him. We are solely responsible for all the shortcomings and faults that we lay at the door of these 'untouchables': it is still open to us to be *Harijan* ourselves but we can only do so by heartily repenting for our sin against them."[2]

Gandhi argued that, "Untouchability is a snake with a thousand mouths through each of which it shows its poisonous fangs. It needs no sanction from Manu or the other ancient law-givers. It has its own local Smriti. Thus, in Almora, a whole class of people, whose occupation is, even according to the *Sanatana Dharma* so-called, innocent, are untouchables. They are all cultivators owning their own holdings. They are called Shilpi, i.e. farmers. Another similar class of people called Boras suffer in the same manner although they do not even eat carrion or take liquor and observe all the rules of sanitation as well as any others. Tradition has condemned them as untouchables".[3]

Gandhi further proclaimed that, "Hinduism that refuses to think and accepts the tradition unquestioningly exposes itself to merited ridicule and worse. Reformers are trying to cope with the evil. I feel, however, that much more drastic methods are needed than are employed to rid Hinduism of the blot. We are needlessly afraid to wound the susceptibilities of orthodoxy. We have to shed the fear, if we expect to end the evil in our own generation. This untouchability naturally recoils on the heads of those who are responsible for it".[4]

The difference, therefore, between the caste system and untouchability is not one of degree, but of kind. An 'untouchable' is outside the pale of respectable society. He is hardly treated as a human being. He is an outcaste hurled into an abyss by his fellow-beings occupying the same platform. The difference, therefore, is somewhat analogous to the difference between heaven and hell.

Gandhi was of the view that untouchability, as it was practiced in Hinduism, was a sin against God and man and was, therefore, like a poison slowly eating into the very vitals of Hinduism. He wrote, "In my opinion, it has no sanction whatsoever in the Hindu Shastras taken as a whole. Untouchability of a healthy kind is undoubtedly to be found in the *Shastras* and it is universal in all religions. It is a rule of sanitation. That will exist to the end of time; but untouchability as we are observing today in India is a hideous thing and wears various forms in various provinces, even in districts. It has degraded both the untouchables and the touchable. It has stunted the growth of nearly 40 million human beings. They are denied even the ordinary amenities of life. The sooner, therefore, it is ended, the better for Hinduism, the better for India, and perhaps better for mankind in general".[5]

Gandhi further elaborated his views, saying that it may not be denied that untouchability is an old institution. But if it is an evil, it cannot be defended on the ground of its antiquity. If the untouchables are outcastes of the Aryan society, so much the worse for that society. And if the Aryans at some stage in their progress regarded a certain class of people as outcastes by way of punishment, there is no reason why that punishment should descend upon their progeny, irrespective of the causes for which their ancestors were punished. It merely demonstrates that the evil cannot be confined and that its deadening effect is all-pervading. He also felt that the existence of untouchability amongst untouchables is an additional reason for cultured Hindu society to rid itself of the curse with the quickest dispatch.

However, Gandhi did not believe the caste system, even as distinguished from *varnashrama*, to be an odious and vicious dogma. It has its limitations and its defects but there is nothing sinful about it, as there is about untouchability, and if it is a by-product of the caste system, it is only in the same sense that an ugly growth is of a body, or weeds of a crop. It is as wrong to destroy caste because of the outcaste, as it would be to destroy a body because of an ugly growth in it or a crop because of the weeds. The outcasteness—in the sense we understand it—has therefore, to be destroyed altogether. It is an abscess to be removed, if the whole system is not to perish. Untouchability is the product, therefore, not of the caste system, but of the distinction of high and low that has crept into Hinduism and is corroding it. The attack on untouchability is, thus, an attack upon this 'high' and 'low'-ness. The moment untouchability goes, the caste system itself will be purified, that is to say, according to Gandhi's dream, it will resolve itself into true *varnadharma*, the four divisions of society, each complementary of the other and none inferior or superior to any other.

Gandhi regarded untouchability as the greatest blot on Hinduism. The idea was not brought home to him by bitter experiences during the South African struggle. It is equally wrong to think-as some people do-that he had taken his view from his study of Christian religious literature. His views date as far back as the time when he was neither enamoured of, nor was acquainted with the Bible or the followers of the Bible.

Gandhi was of the firm view that the removal of untouchability was much more than building a temple of brick and mortar. Hindus must bleed for it, must pay for it. They must be prepared to for the sake of wife, children and all for the sake of removing the curse.[6]

Gandhi also believed that to remove untouchability is a penance that caste Hindus owe to Hinduism and to themselves. The purification required is not of 'untouchables' but of the so-called superior castes. There is no vice, that is, special to the 'untouchables', not even dirt and insanitation. It is our arrogance which blinds us, superior Hindus, to our own blemishes and magnifies those of our down-trodden brethren whom we have suppressed and whom we keep under suppression. Religions, like nations, are being weighed in balance. Gandhi further emphasized, God's grace and revelation are the monopoly of no race or nation. They descend equally upon all who wait upon God. That religion and that nation will be blotted out of the face of the earth, which pins its faith to injustice, untruth or violence. God is light, not darkness, God is love, not hate, God is Truth, not untruth. God alone is great. We, His creatures, are but dust. Let us be humble and recognize the place of the lowliest of His creatures. Krishna honoured Sudama in his rags as he honoured no one else. Love is the root of religion'[7].

Gandhi told Congressmen that 'by' making removal of untouchability a plank in our platform, we assert our belief that untouchability is not only not a part and parcel of Hinduism but a corroding and sinful superstition, which has infected Hinduism, and that it is the bounden duty of every Hindu to strive for its abolition. Every Hindu, therefore, who considers it a sin, should atone for it by fraternizing with untouchables, touching them in a spirit of love and service, deeming himself purified by that touch, redressing their grievances, helping them patiently to overcome ignorance and other evils due to the slavery of ages and inspiring other Hindus to do likewise. When one visualizes the removal of untouchability from this spiritual standpoint, its material and political results sink into insignificance in his eyes, and one befriends the so-called untouchables regardless of such results'.[8] Seekers after truth will never waste a thought on the material consequences of their quest, which is not a matter of policy with them but something interwoven with the very texture of their lives. This is equally true of the removal of untouchability. Removal of untouchability spelt for Gandhi the breaking down of barriers between man and man and between the various orders of being. Such barriers can be found erected everywhere in the world, but Gandhi was mainly concerned with the untouchability which had received religious sanction in India and reduced lakhs and crores of human beings to a state bordering on slavery.[9]

Gandhi also believed that the cause of *Harijans* and Hinduism will not be served by the methods of rabble. He found the exercise to be perhaps the biggest religious reform movement in India, if not in the world, involving as it did the well-being of nearly forty million human beings living in serfdom. One had to win them by love, by self-sacrifice, by perfect self-restraint, by letting the purity of one's life produce its own silent effect upon their hearts. It could be done by having faith in truth and love converting the opponents to one's own way.

Untouchability, Gandhi was convinced, could not be removed even by the force of law. It could only be removed when the majority of Hindus realized that this is a crime against God and man and feel ashamed of it. In other words, it was to be a process of conversion, i.e. purification, of the Hindu heart. Gandhi felt that the aid of law has to be invoked when it hinders or interferes with the progress of the reform as when—in spite of the willingness of the trustees and the temple-going public—the law prohibits the opening of a particular temple.

Gandhiji maintained that the spirit of untouchability must have been a product of our lowest ebb. He called it a curse for society. So long as this curse prevails in the society, people will be committing crimes. Further, one finds that according to Gandhi, the idea of untouchability does not have any religious sanction. Religion did not provide any room for this. He reinforced and emphasized, "Untouchability is not a sanction of religion, it is a device of Satan." He often said and wrote, "I regard untouchability as the greatest blot of Hinduism." [10] He further emphasized, "It is against the shastras".

Gandhiji tried to preach the gospel of love to the whole world. According to him, all men—irrespective of their caste affiliations—belong to one God and were his expressions. He said and believed that removal of this great sin of untouchability meant, "love for, and service of, the whole world, and thus merges into *ahimsa*. Removal of untouchability spells the breaking down of barriers between man and man and between the various orders of Being. We find such barriers erected everywhere in the world."

Gandhi was an honest follower of non-violence. So, Gandhi sought to change the hearts of the caste Hindus by moral pressure. He strived hard to force on the Indian Conscience the problem of untouchability as an issue of national concern. Although, the measures of legally abolishing untouchability were adopted in the Constituent Assembly. Gandhi never advocated legal measures. He did feel that all changes must come voluntarily from the heart. Gandhi, no doubt, anathematized 'untouchability' with all the force of his spirit. His crystal earnestness was proved by the life he lived and the works he did. Work was worship for him "I am an 'untouchable' by adoption" said Gandhi to Ambedkar during the crucial talks before the Poona Pact of 1932 over the representation of Scheduled Castes and Scheduled Tribes in the legislatures then to come under the Government of India Act, 1935. "My greatest worry", he said then, as he had said repeatedly before and since "is the ignorance and poverty of the masses of India and the way in which they have been neglected by the classes, especially the neglect of the *Harijans* by the Hindus. We are custodians of a great religion and yet have been guilty of a crime, which constitutes our greatest shame. Had I not been a believer in the inscrutable ways of providence, a sensitive man like me would have been a raving maniac."[11] It was with this conviction that Gandhi could say unconventional things, such as, a '*Bhangi* does for society what a mother does for a baby'. He could also match such words with action, as he did when he adopted an 'untouchable' girl as his daughter. From time to time, he used to express his desire that independent India should have on 'untouchable' woman as its President a desire yet to be fulfilled.

Gandhi was strongly committed to a social philosophy which consolidated his faith in persuasion and he opposed what he called "reform by compulsion". He insisted that the "*satyagrahis* must stoop to conquer" and wanted "to set even the most orthodox and the most bigoted at ease" during the Travencore

Movement 1924-25 for unfettered use of roads to the temple by the 'untouchables'. It was Gandhi's idea of "the beauty of compromise" that led to a settlement, hailed by Gandhi himself as a 'miracle' adding only eight furlongs or so to roads free for all (including untouchables) which led to the creation of a new and more promising atmosphere for social change.

Gandhi believed in the traditional concept of Varna system cleansed of untouchability, in which untouchables would be '*harijans*' and their unclean work would be accepted as honourable. It is because, though an ardent champion for removing untouchability, he sought to do so within the Hindu Chaturvarna framework. Gandhi said time and again that untouchability is the sin of the Hindus and they must purify themselves by paying the debt they owe to their suppressed brothers and sister. Hinduism has sinned in giving sanction to untouchability. It has degraded us, made us pariahs. Even the Mussalmans have caught the sinful contagion form us".

He sought to emphasize that in Hinduism there is no sanction for treating a single human being as untouchable. In the estimation of a Brahmin, knowing and living his religion, a Shudra is as good as himself. The *Bhagavad-Gita* has nowhere taught that a *Chandala* is in any way inferior to a Brahmin. A Brahmin ceases to be a Brahmin immediately he becomes insolent and considers himself a superior being. India owes a deep debt to the Brahmins who voluntarily sacrificed themselves for the betterment of all. It was Brahmins who have called God Servant of Servants, the Purifier of the Fallen. It was Brahmins who taught that the prostitute and the *Chandala* could attain *moksha* if she or he only purified her or his heart[12].

It was, therefore, Gandhi believed, the moral duty of all Hindus to see that the 'untouchables' do not feel that they are despised or looked down upon. Let them not be offered leavings from our plates for their subsistence, he exhorted the Hindus and questioned them as to how could one accord differential treatment to any person, be he a *Brahmin* or *Bhangi*, who worships the same God and keeps his body and soul pure and clean? He warned them that one would have to regard himself as having sinned if one gave to a *Bhangi* unclean food from the leavings from the kitchen or failed to render him personal assistance when he was in need.

British Prime Minister MacDonald proposed separate electrorate for the Untouchables at the Round Table Conference, Gandhi put a firm resistance. He argued endlessly that Muslims, Sikhs or Christians will remain so for all times, but why would the Untouchables remain untouchables in the future too, or should they? His suggestion was to grant them adequate concessions to ameliorate their condition and even reservations to ensure their representation in the Councils and other elected bodies but no separation from the general electorate, which if decided, he would oppose with his life, Gandhi had warned.

In a few months when the proposal for separate electorate for the untouchable Scheduled Castes was moved in MacDonald's Communal Award, Gandhi announced his decision to undertake a fast till death, unless this provision was changed. He explained that his primary concern was not merely to oppose this particular administrative-cum-constitutional measure that the British Government was going to introduce in India[13]. His principal concern was the inhuman odium of the practice of untouchability which cried for its immediate abolition, together with other reforms in Hindu society, on the one hand, and the excuse and the justification it provided to the colonial power to play its game of disrupting and fragmenting Hindu society on the other.

He was for granting whatever concessions the Depressed Classes leaders wanted provided they strengthened the integration of Hindu society in general rather than weakening it. With the fast continuing and the Mahatma's life at stake, there was a tidal wave of public opinion, which battered against hard-core Hindu Conservatism; hundreds of temples were opened to the untouchables and a large number of Hindu leaders pledged to do away with the centuries—old discriminations practiced against the untouchables[14]. In the bargain the Scheduled Castes were offered almost double the number of reserved seats than that promised in the British White Paper. In the event the agreement was clinched, the British Government agreed to make the necessary amendments in the White Paper if the Scheduled Castes and the Hindu sides were mutually satisfied on their agreement. It was then that the Mahatma broke his fast on 25th September, the seventh day of his fast unto death. Of all the large number of Indian leaders who had expressed their anguish at the impending threat to the Mahatma's life, it was Rabindranath Tagore who said that "untouchability was a serious enough blemish on the face of Hinduism which justified even putting to risk the Mahatma's precious life for its removal"[15].

Parallel with the signing of the accord on the issue of representation of the Scheduled Castes and modalities of elections (popularly known as the Poona Pact), Gandhi insisted from his Yeravda prison that the Congress, Liberals, and the Hindu Mahasabha leaders also publicly announce their acceptance of another declaration the text of which he drafted himself. This was adopted on 25 September 1932 at a joint public meeting held in Bombay. The text was as follows:

> "This Conference resolves that henceforth, amongst Hindus, no one shall be regarded as an untouchable by reason of his birth, and that those who have been so regarded hitherto will have the same right as other

> Hindus in regard to the use of public wells, pubic schools, roads and all other public institutions. This right shall have statutory recognition at the first opportunity and shall be one of the earliest Acts of the *Swaraj* Parliament, if it shall not have received such recognition before that time.
>
> It is further agreed that it shall be the duty of all Hindu leaders to secure, by every legitimate and peaceful means, an early removal of all social disabilities now imposed by custom upon the so-called untouchable classes, including the bar in respect of admission to temples".

It is to be noted that Gandhi himself considered this declaration of historic significance and on several occasions in the course of the following decade and a half (till the transfer of power, that is) he reminded his fellow Hindus that this was a standing commitment. Regrettably, however, neither any broad convention of Hindu society nor the Congress-led Ministries that were in office from 1937 to 1939 took any formal or legal step to implement the essence of this declaration.

Although the British Government, honouring the compromise agreement, withdrew its original proposal and accepted what came to be commonly known as the Poona Accord, there were all-round murmurings of perceived grievances on a large scale. In Bengal specially, the grumbling against the Communal Award generally as also against those aspects that emerged as a result of the Poona Accord, was particularly vociferous and organized. It was at this stage that the orthodox Hindu campaign went on a general offensive on the need to preserve the traditional customs of Hindu society on the one hand, and on the other, in its fight to ensure that the Hindus received their hitherto unquestioned lion's share of the concessions the British were about to grant in India.

Gandhi sought to evolve a new strategy and a new slogan that would enable him to mobilize the people, first of all the Hindu majority in their entirety. That would not only fully overcome the *Savarna-Avarna* divide but having done so would so integrate them, breaking down the hierarchical division of high and low in the Hindu society, that it would clear the path for communal unity too, so believed Gandhi. He watched the situation: the depressed classes movement was making very slow progress, but the orthodox camp's propaganda was becoming increasingly bold and offensive.

More than a year passed (14 months) between the Poona Pact and the start of the campaign during which Gandhi, apart from speaking at some meetings and talking to innumerable colleagues and other leaders, wrote every frequently on the question of untouchability. In fact, he declared several times that this was the one issue that was then commanding all his attention. He started new journals reflective of the new campaign—*Harijan*—first in English (February, 1993) followed by other editions in Gujarati, Hindi, Bengali, Tamil, and other, all at short intervals.

Gandhi's intense and passionate campaign against untouchability in which he engaged himself from November 1933 to August 1934 and which took him not only to almost all parts of British India but also to a large number of the adjoining Princely states. The Gandhi campaign was a great social-historical event in India. It represented a great social turmoil. This campaign, therefore, revealed and manifested all the contradictions of our social reality.

In a nutshell, Gandhi's strategy for tackling the evil of untouchability was as follows:

- He called untouchables as *Harijans* that is 'the children of God'.

- He tried to spread awareness against the evils of untouchability by actively involving the upper castes in order to change their mindset through awareness. In his efforts to do so, Gandhi started newspapers—*Harijan* in English, *Harijan Sewak* in Hindi and *Harijanbandhu* in Gujarati.
- He established the Harijan Sewak Sangh devoted to the uplift of *Harijans.* Even in his ashram *Harijans* were given due respect and they were at par with rest of the other inanimate.
- He conducted 'Harijan Tours' throughout India to spread the message against untouchability and collected money for their betterment.
- Gandhi supported the movement for throwing open place of worship and temples for *Harijans.*
- Gandhi lent support to the *Vaikom Satyagraha* in Kerela, which was organized for allowing the use of road near temple for untouchables.
- Being a non-violent person, Gandhi was not averse to taking the help of law and constitutional means. Some of the inspired legislators introduced Bills aimed at removing the disabilities placed on *Harijans* by some Provincial Goverments and in some provisions of law, from entering temples. In the 1930s, two Bills were awaiting Viceroy's sanction, one for introduction in the Central Legislative Assembly by Ranga Iyer and other for introduction in Madras Council by Subbaroyan. Gandhi gave wide publicity to these Bills and requested legislators to give their full support to them.
- Gandhi entered into dialogue with Narayan Guru of Kerela and the Self-Respect Movement led by E.V. Ramaswamy.

- Gandhi's entire life was dedicated to the cause of *Harijans*. His efforts were unique unparaller and in humans history. He striked the root of untouchability.

Gandhi on Untouchability

So far as *Harijans* are concerned every Hindu should make a common cause with them and befriend them in their awful isolation. (*Source*: *Gandhi Diary*, 1998).

Untouchability means pollution by the touch of certain persons by reason of their birth in a particular state or family. It is an excrescence. In the guise of religion, it is always in the way, and erupts religion. [–Form *Yeravda Mandir*. p. 31.]

There is an ineffaceable blot that Hinduism today carries with it. I have declined to believe that it has been handed to us from immemorial times. I think that this miserable, wretched, enslaving spirit of untouchability must have come to us when we were in the cycle of our lives at our lowest ebb… That any person should be considered untouchable in this sacred land passes one's comprehension.

[– *Speeches and Writings of Mahatma Gandhi*: p. 387.]

Untouchability is a sin against God and man. There is no warrant in the *Shastras* for untouchability as we practice it today

[*Harijan*: March 2, 1934.]

I consider untouchability to be a heinous crime against humanity. It is not a sign of self-restraint, but an arrogant assumption of superiority. [*Young India*: December 8, 1920.]

Untouchability is a snake with a thousand mouths, through each of which it shows its poisonous fangs. It defied definition. It needs no sanction from Manu or the other ancient lawgivers.

[*Young India*: July 11, 1927.]

Untouchability is blot upon Hinduism and must be removed at any cost. Untouchability is a poison, which, if we do not get rid of it in time, will destroy Hinduism.

[*Harijan*: June 20, 1936.]

And why do I say that untouchability is a curse, a blot and a powerful poison that will destroy Hinduism? It is repugnant to our sense of humanity to consider a single human being as untouchability by birth. If you were to examine the scriptures of the world and the conduct of peoples other than Hindus, you do not find any parallel to the untouchability.

[*Harijan*: June 20, 1936.]

I believe that if untouchability is really rooted out, it will not only purge Hinduism of a terrible blot, but its repercussion will be worldwide. My fight against untouchability is a fight against the impure in humanity. [*Mahatma*: Vol. III, p. 203.]

What I want, what I am living for and what I should delight in dying for is the eradication of untouchability, root and branch.

[*Mahatma*: Vol. III. p. 205.]

Removal of untouchability means love for, and service of the whole world, and thus merges into *Ahimsa*. Removal of untouchability spells the breaking down of barriers between man and man, and between the various orders of Being.

[From *Yeravda Mandir*: p. 33.]

Removal of untouchability means not merely touching the *Harijans* (untouchables), but also looking upon them as our own kith and kin; in other words, treating them in the same way as we would our own brothers and sisters. None is high, none low.
[*Bapu-ke-Ashirvad*, November 28, 1944.]

They are not untouchables, we are untouchables. They eat and drink and think and feel even as we do. If a sum total of their virtues and vices and the privileges they are denied were to be made and compared with our virtues and vices and the privileges we enjoy and deny to them, I am sure in God's books we should find our debit side far heavier than theirs.

[*Young India*: May, 13, 1926.]

Untouchability is repugnant to reason and to the instinct of mercy, pity, and love. No man can consider another man inferior to himself. He must consider every man as his blood brother. It is the cardinal principle of every religion.

[*Speeches and Writings of Mahatma Gandhi*: p. 930.]

It is a sin to believe that anyone else is inferior or superior to ourselves. We are all equal. It is the touch of sin that pollutes us, and never that of a human being. None are high and none are low for who would devote his life to service. The distinction between high and low is a blot on Hinduism, which we must obliterate. [*The Diary of Mahadev Desai*: p. 286.]

The distinction of high and low is at the bottom of untouchability. So long as the idea of high and low is not abolished, untouchability cannot be said to have been abolished.

[*Conversations of Gandhiji*: p. 60.]

In battling against untouchability and in dedicating myself to that battle, I have no less an ambition than to see a complete regeneration of humanity. It may be mere dream, as unreal as the silver in the seashell. It is not so to me while the dream lasts, and, in the words of Romain Rolland: "Victory lies not in realization of the goal, but in a relentless pursuit after it."

[*Harijan*, March 25, 1933.]

In dealing with the monster of untouchability, my own innermost desire is not that the brotherhood of Hindus only may be achieved, but it essentially is that the brotherhood of man—be he Hindu, Mussalman, Christian, Parsi of Jew—may be realized. [*Harijan*, February 16, 1934.]

I do want *Moksha*. I do not want to be reborn. But if I have to be reborn, I should be born as an untouchable, so that o may share their sorrows, sufferings, and the affronts leveled at them, in order that I may endeavour to free myself and them from that miserable condition.... If I should die with any of my desires unfulfilled, with my service of the untouchables unfinished, with my Hinduism unfulfilled, I may be born again amongst the untouchables to bring my Hinduism to fulfilment.

[*Harijan*, September 12, 1936.]

Gandhi rightly said: "I do not want to be reborn. But if I have to be reborn, I should be born an untouchable, so that I may share their sorrows, sufferings, and the affronts leveled at them, in order that I may endeavour to free myself and them from that miserable condition. I, therefore, pray that if I should be born again I should do so not as a Brahmin, Kshatriya, Vaishya, Or Shudra, but as an Atishudra".

Summing Up

Gandhi is believed to have advocated that people should continue in their ancestral occupations and it is also alleged that he advised the *Dalits* to nurture a relationship with the upper castes analogous to that of the black Uncle Tom towards the latter's former white masters.[17] Nothing could be farther from truth and from what Gandhi really stood and campaigned for.

What is remarkable about Gandhi is that instead of falsely glorifying the past, he in fact, infused the past with his very modern ideas of truth, justice, fearlessness, fraternity, absence of hierarchy, and dignity of the individual values which he thought were essential for the revivification of our ancient but also decadent society. Thus, he was most unsparing in condemning all that was reactionary, oppressive and exploitative in our traditional customs, characterizing them as the excretions of the historical process, and called for their absolute elimination.

Notes

1. *Young India*, 26-12-1924. and also *Harijan*, 28.9.1934.
2. *Young India*, 6.8.1931.
3. Tendulkar, D.G., *The Mahatma*, Vol. IV, New Delhi, Publications Divisions, 1952, pp. 125-26.
4. *Speeches and Writings of Mahatma Gandhi*, Vol. II, pp. 336-44.
5. *Harijan*, 9.10.1937, p. 292.
6. Iyer, Raghvan, *Political and Moral Thoughts of Mahatma Gandhi*, New York: Oxford University, 1973.
7. See for details, *Speeches and Writings of Mahatma Gandhi*, Vol. II, pp. 340-54.
8. *Young India*, April 27, 1921.
9. *Young India*, September 18, 1930.
10. *Young India*, January 21, 1926.
11. Tendulkar, *op. cit.*, Vol. IV, pp. 125-26.
12. *Young India*, May 11, 1921.
13. *Speeches and Writings of Mahatma Gandhi*, Vol. II, pp. 336-44.
14. *Harijan*, 9.10.1937.
15. Iyer, Raghvan, *op. cit.*
16. Gandhi, M.K., From Yirvada Mandir, Ahmedabad, Navajivan Publishing House, 1932, p. 31.
17. Ram, Jagivan, Mahatma Gandhi and Social Change in S. Radhakrishnan (ed.), *Mahatma Gandhi—100 Years*, New Delhi, Gandhi Peace Foundation, 1968, pp. 156-160.

PART TWO
STATEMENT ON UNTOUCHABILITY

2

Statement on Untouchability[1]-I

November 4, 1932

For reasons over which I had no control I have not been able to deal with the question of untouchability, as I had fully intended to after the breaking of the fast. The Government having now granted me permission to carry on public propaganda in connection with the work, I am able to deal with the numerous correspondents who have been writing to me either in criticism of the Yeravda Pact, or to seek guidance, or to know my views about the different questions that arise in the course of the campaign against untouchability. In this preliminary statement I propose to confine myself to the salient questions only, deferring for the time being other questions which do not call for immediate disposal.

I take up first the question of the possibility of my resuming the fast. Some correspondents contend that the fast savours of coercion and should not have been undertaken at all and that, therefore, it should never be resumed. Some others have argued that there is no warrant in Hindu religion, or any religion for that matter, for a fast like mine. I do not propose to deal with the religious aspect. Suffice it to say that it was at God's call that I embarked upon the last fast and it would be at His call that it would be resumed, if it ever is. But when it was first undertaken, it was undoubtedly for removal of untouchability, root and branch. That it took the form it did was no choice of mine. The Cabinet decision precipitated the crisis of my life, but I knew that the revocation of the British Cabinet's decision was to be but the begining of the end. A tremendous force could not be set in motion merely in order to alter a political decision, unless it had behind it a much deeper meaning even unknown to its authors. The people affected instinctively recognized that meaning and responded.

Perhaps no man within living memory has travelled so often from one end of India to the other or has penetrated so many villages and come into contact with so many millions as I have. They have all known my life. They have known that I have recognized no barriers between 'untouchables' and 'touchables' or caste and outcaste. They have heard me speak often in their own tongues denouncing untouchability in unmeasured terms, describing it as a curse and a blot upon Hinduism. With rare exceptions, at hundreds of these mass meetings or at private meetings in all parts of India, there has been no protest against my presentation of the case against untouchability.

Crowds have passed resolutions denouncing untouchability and pledging themselves to remove it from their midst and they have on innumerable occasions called God as witness to their pledge and asked for His blessing that He may give them strength to carry out their pledge. It was against these millions that my fast was undertaken and it was their spontaneous love that brought about a transformation inside of five days and brought into being the Yeravda Pact. And it will be against them that the fast will be resumed if that Pact is not carried out by them in its fullness. The Government are now practically out of it.

Their part of the obligation they fulfilled promptly. The major part of the resolutions of the Yeravda Pact has to be fulfilled by these millions, the so-called caste Hindus, who have flocked to the meetings I have described. It is they who have to embrace the suppressed brethren and sisters as their very own, whom they have to invite to their temples, to their homes, to their schools. The 'untouchables' in the villages should be made to feel that their shackles have been broken, that they are in no way inferior to their fellow-villagers, that they are worshippers of the same God as other villagers, and are entitled to the same rights and privileges that the latter enjoy.

But if these vital conditions of the Pact are not carried out by caste Hindus, could I possibly live to face God and man? I ventured even to tell Dr. Ambedkar, Rao Bahadur Raja and other friends belonging to the suppressed group that they should regard me as a hostage for the due fulfilment by caste Hindus of the conditions of the Pact. The fast, if it has to come, will not be for the coercion of those who are opponents of the reform, but it will be intended to sting into action those who have been my comrades or who have taken pledges for the removal of untouchability. If they believe their pledge, or if they never meant to abide by them, and their Hinduism was a mere camouflage, I should have no interest left in life. My fast, therefore, ought not to affect the opponents of reform, nor even fellow-workers and the millions who have led me to believe that they were with me and the Congress in the campaign against untouchability, if the latter have on second thoughts come to the conclusion that untouchability is not after all a crime against God and humanity.

In my opinion, fasting for purification of self and others is an age-long institution and it will subsist so long as man believes in God. It is the prayer to the Almighty from an anguished heart. But whether my argument is wise or foolish, I cannot be dislodged from my position so long as I do not see the folly or the error of it. It will be resumed only in obedience to the inner voice, and only if there is manifest breakdown of the Yeravda Pact, owing to the criminal neglect of caste Hindus to implement its conditions. Such neglect would mean a betrayal of Hinduism. I should not care to remain its living witness.

There is another fast which is a near possibility and that is in connection with the opening of the Guruvayur temple in Kerala. It was at my urgent request that Sjt. Kelappan suspended his fast for three months, a fast that had well-nigh brought him to death's door. I would be in honour bound to fast with him if on or before the first January next that temple is not opened to the 'untouchables'precisely on the same terms as the 'touchables', and if it becomes necessary for Sjt. Kelappan to resume his fast. I have been obliged to dwell at some length upon these possible fasts because of the receipt of hot correspondence from two or three quarters. Co-workers, however, should not be agitated over the possiblity. To become unnerved over a prospect one would not like face very often results in its materializing. The best way of averting it is for all affected by it to put forth their whole strength into the work that would render the occurrence impossible.

Correspondents have asked whether inter-dining and intermarriage are part of the movement against untouchability. In my opinion they are not. They touch the caste men equally with the outcastes. It is, therefore, not obligatory on an anti-untouchability worker to devote himself or herself to inter-dining and intermarriage reform. Personally, I am of opinion that this reform is coming sooner than we expect. Restriction on inter-caste dining and inter-caste marriage is no part of Hindu religion. It is a social custom which crept into Hinduism when perhaps it was in its decline, and was then meant perhaps to be temporary protection against disintegration of Hindu society, and emphasis on them has turned the attention of mass mind from the fundamentals which are vital to life's growth. Wherever, therefore, people voluntarily take part in functions where 'touchables' and 'untouchables', Hindus and in non-Hindus are invited to join dinner parties, I welcome them as a healthy sign. But I should never dream of making this reform, however, desirable in itself it may be, part of an all-India reform which has been long overdue.

Untouchability in the form we all know it is a canker eating into the very vitals of Hinduism. Dining and marriage restrictions stunt Hindu society. I think the distinction is fundamental. It would be unwise in a hurricane capmaign to overweight and thus endanger the main issue. It may even amount to a breach of faith with the masses to call upon them suddenly to view the removal of untouchability in a light different from what they have been taught to believe it to be. On the one hand, therefore, whilst inter-dining may go on where the public is itself ready for it, it should not be part of the India-wide campaign.

I have letters, some of them angrily worded, from those who style themselves sanatanists. For them untouchability, is the essence of Hinduism. Some of them regard me as a renegade. Some others consider that I have imbibed notions against untouchability and the like from Christianity and Islam. Some again quote scriptures in defence of untouchability. To these I have promised a reply through this statement. I would venture, therefore, to tell these correspondents that I claim myself to be a sanatanist. Their definition of a sanatanist is obviously different from mine. For me *Sanatan Dharma* is the vital faith handed down from generations belonging even to prehistoric period and based upon the Vedas and the writings that followed them.

For me the Vedas are as indefinable as God and Hinduism. It would be only partially true to say that the Vedas are the four books which one finds in print. These books are themselves remnants of the discourses left by the unknown seers. Those of later generations added to these original treasures according to their lights. There then arose a great and lofty-minded man, the composer of the *Gita.* He gave to the Hindu world a synthesis of Hindu religion at once deeply philosophical and yet easily to be understood by any unsophisticated seeker. It is the one open book to every Hindu who will care to study it, and if all the other scriptures were reduced to ashes, the seven hundred verses of this imperishable booklet are quite enough to tell one what Hinduism is and how one can live up to it. And I claim to be a sanatanist because for forty years I have been seeking literally to live up to the teachings of that book. Whatever, is contrary to its main theme I reject as un-Hindu. It excludes no faith and no teacher. It gives me great joy to be able to say that I have studied the Bible, the Koran, Zend Avesta and the other scriptures of the world with thesame reverence that I have given to the *Gita.* This reverent reading has strengthened my faith in the *Gita.* They have broadened my outlook and, therefore, my Hinduism. Lives of Zoroaster, Jesus and Mohammed, as I have understood them, have illumined many a passage in the *Gita.* What, therefore, these sanatani friends have hurled against me as a taunt has been to me a source of consolation. I take pride in calling myself a Hindu becuase I find the term broad enough not merely to tolerate but to assimilate the teachings of prophets from all the four corners of the earth. I find no warrant for untouchability in this book of life. On the contrary it compels me, by an appeal to my reason and a more penetrating appeal to my heart, in language that has a magnetic touch about it, to believe that all life is one and that it is through God and must return to Him.

According to *Sanatan Dharma* taught by that venerable Mother[2], life does not consist in outward rites and ceremonial, but it consists in the uttermost inner purification and merging oneself, body, soul and mind, in the divine essence. I have gone to the masses in their millions with this message of the *Gita* burnt into my life. And they have listened to me, I am quite sure, not for any political wisdom or for eloquence, but because they have instinctively recognized me as one of them, as one belonging to their faith. And as days have gone by, my belief has grown stronger and stronger that I could not be wrong in claiming to belong to *Sanatan Dharma*, and if God wills it, He will let me seal that claim with my death.

—*The Epic Fast*, pp. 311-7.

Notes

1. Following the lifting of restrictions by the Government on Gandhiji's interviews and his carrying on propaganda in connection with anti-untouchability work, Gandhiji issued a series of statements to the Press. This is the first of them.
2. *Bhagavad Gita*

3

Statement on Untouchability-II

November 5, 1932

A correspondent, in spite of having received liberal education suggests that before *Harijans* are put on a level with caste Hindus, they should become fit for such reception, shed their dirty habits, give up eating carrion; another goes the length of saying that *Bhangis* and *Chamars* who are engaged in what he considers are 'dirty occupations' should give them up. These critics forget that caste men are responsible for whatever bad habits are to be observed amongst the *Harijans*. The so-called higher castes have deprived them of facilities for keeping themselves clean and also the incentive for doing so. As for the occupations of scavenging and tanning, they are no more dirty than many other occupations I can name. What may be admitted is that these occupations like several others are carried on in a dirty manner. That again is due to the high-handed indifference and criminal neglect of the 'high castes'. I can say from personal experience that both scavenging and tanning can be done in a perfectly healthy and clean manner. Every mother is a scavenger in regard to her own children and every student of modern medicine is a tanner in as much as he has to dissect and skin human carcases. But we consider theirs to be sacred occupations. I submit that the ordinary scavengers' and tanners' occupations are no less sacred and no less useful than those of mothers and medical men. We shall go wrong if caste men regard themselves as patrons distributing favours to the *Harijans*. Whatever is done now by the caste Hindus for the *Harijans* will be but a tardy reparation for the wrongs done to them for generations, and if now they have to be received in their existing state, as they must be received, it is a well-deserved punishment for the past guilt. But there is this certain satisfaction that the very act of receiving them with open hearts would be a sufficient incentive to cleanliness, and the caste men will for their own comfort and convenience provide *Harijans* with facilities for keeping themselves clean.

It is well to remind ourselves of what wrongs we have heaped upon the devoted heads of the *Harijans*. Socially they are lepers. Economically they are worse than slaves. Religiously they are denied entrance to places we miscall 'houses of God'. They are denied the use, on the same terms as the caste men, of public roads, public schools, public hospitals, public wells, public taps, public parks and so on, and in some cases their approach within a measured distance is a social crime, and in some other rare enough cases their very sight is an offence. They are relegated for their residence to the worst quarters of cities or villages where they practically get no social services. Caste Hindu lawyers and doctors will not serve them as they do other members of society. Brahmins will not officiate at their religious functions. The wonder is that they are at all able to eke out an existence or that they still remain within the Hindu fold. They are too downtrodden to rise in revolt against their suppressors.

I have recalled these tragic and shameful facts in order to make the workers vividly realize the implications of the Yeravda Pact. It is only ceaseless effort that can raise these downtrodden fellow-beings from degradation, purify Hinduism, and raise the whole Hindu society and with it the whole of India.

Let us not be stunned by this simple recital of the wrongs. If the demonstration during the last week was a genuine expression of repentance on the part of caste Hindus, all will be well, and every *Harijan* will soon feel the glow of freedom. But before this much desired end can be achieved the message of freedom will have to be carried to the remotest village. Indeed the work in the village is far more difficult than in the big cities where it is possible quickly to mobilize public opinion. Now that there is the All-India Antiuntouchability League, workers should work in co-ordination with that League. And here I would like to recall what Dr. Ambedkar told me. He said, "Let there be no repetition of the old method when the reformer claimed to know more of the requirements of his victims than the victims themselves", and, therefore, he added "tell your workers to ascertain from the representatives of the *Harijans* what their first need is and how they would like it to be satisfied. Joint refreshments are good enough by way of demonstration, but they may be overdone. There is a flavour of patronage about them. I would not attend them by myself. The more dignified procedure would be to invite us to ordinary social functions without any fuss. Even temple-entry, good and necessary as it is, may wait. The crying need is the raising of the economic status and decent behaviour in the daily contact." I must not repeat here some of the harrowing details given by him from his own bitter experiences. I felt the force of his remarks. I hope every one of my readers will do likewise.

Many suggestions have been sent to me for adoption by the reformers. One is a repetition of what Swami Shraddhanandji used to repeat so often, namely, that every Hindu should have in his home a *Harijan* who would be for all practical purposes a member of the family. The second comes from a non-Hindu friend deeply interested in India's welfare. He says that every well-to-do Hindu should bear the expense of giving, if possible under his own observation, higher education to a Harijan young man or girl so that these after finishing their education might work for the uplift of fellow-*Harijans*. Both the suggestions are worthy of consideration and adoption. I would ask all who have made fruitful suggestions to pass them on to the newly established League. Correspondents should recognize my limitations.

From behind the prison gates, I can only tender advice to the League and the people. I can take no part in the real execution of plans. They should also recognize that my opinions, based as they must be on insufficient data, and often on second-hand information, are liable to revision in the light of new facts and should, therefore, be received with caution.

Though it is now past history I would devote a paragraph to the objection raised by a correspondent and even voiced in suppressed tones in the Press. Referring to the political part of the Pact they ask, 'What have you gained by it? The *Harijans* have surely got much more than the Prime Minister gave'. Well, that is exactly the gain. My objection to the decision was that it gave stone instead of bread. This Pact has given bits of bread. I personally would have rejoiced with Dr. Moonje if the *Harijans* had got all the seats allotted to the Hindus. That would have been the greatest gain to caste Hindus and Hinduism.

What I wanted and what I still want is their complete merger in the caste Hindus and the latter's in the former. It is my deliberate opinion, not likely to be altered by any fresh fact that may come to light, that the more the suppressors give to the suppressed the more they gain.

They gain *pro tanto* discharge from overdue debts. Unless the caste Hindus approach the question in that humble, penitent, religious and right spirit, the remaining part of the Pact will never be observed in the spirit that seemed to pervade Hindu society during the fast week.

I would like to tender my congratulations to those Princes who have opened their State temples to the *Harijans* and have otherwise proclaimed banishment of untouchability from their States. If I may say it, they have thereby done some penance on their own behalf and their people's. I hope that the Hindus residing in these States will carry out the terms of these proclamations and so fraternize with them as to make the *Harijans* feel that they never were the despised outcastes of Hindu humanity. We are too near the scene of tragedy to realize that this canker of untouchability has travelled far beyond its prescribed limits and has sapped the foundations of the whole nation.

The touch-me-not spirit pervades the atmosphere. If, therefore, this white ant is touched at its source, I feel sure that we shall soon forget the differences with regard to caste and caste and religion and religion and begin to believe that even as all Hindus are one and indivisible, so are all Hindus, Mussalmans, Sikhs, Parsis, Jews and Christians, branches of the same parent tree. Though religions are many, Religion is one. That is the lesson I would have us learn from the campaign against untouchability. And we will learn it, if we prosecute it in the religious spirit with a determination that will not be resisted.

—*The Epic Fast*, pp. 318-22

4

Statement on Untouchability-III

November 7, 1932

A correspondent whom I know well and who is in sympathy with the movement against untouchability, though he does not accept the whole of the programme, wrote a long letter in Hindi from which I condense the following:

I fear that the campaign is not being kept within bounds in all parts of the country. I understand in some cases those who claim to be workers in the cause are making use of questionable methods such as resorting to abuse of adherents of the old order, and pouring ridicule on sacred names. Anyone who dares to analyse your sayings or writings or to oppose the extreme forms that the campaign is taking, immediately becomes a butt of ridicule and is labelled a traitor to his religion and even threatened with dire consequences. They do not seem to care for the material or moral welfare of the outcastes. They think that their effort begins and ends with promiscuous dinners and marching crowds of *Harijans* to temples even in defiance of the wishes to the contrary of the trustees. I am sure you do not want the movement to degenerate into mere spectacular demonstrations calculated merely to wound the feelings of the orthodox without doing the least service to the *Harijans*.

Out of nearly a hundred letters on untouchability received by me during the past month this is the first letter complaining of workers' conduct bordering on violence. I, however, felt the necessity for giving publicity to the complaint, if only out of regard for my correspondent's warning to workers. I know he will not indulge in wilful exaggeration. There can be no compulsion in matters of religion, I should say in any matter. The public know my very strong views against violence in any shape or form against anyone, no matter what his caste, creed, or nationality may be.

Let those in charge of the movement, therefore, understand that even in their impatience to save me from the prospective fast they may not force the pace by adopting questionable methods. If they do so, they will merely hasten my end. It would be living death for me to witness the degeneration of the movement on whose behalf, as I believe, God had prompted that little fast. The cause of the *Harijans* and Hinduism will not be served by methods of rabble. This is perhaps the biggest religious reform movement in India, if not in the world, involving as it does the well-being of nearly sixty million human beings living in serfdom.

The orthodox section that disapproves of this is entitled to every courtesy and consideration. We have to win them by love, by self-sacrifice, by perfect self-restraint, and by letting purity of our lives produce its own silent effect upon their hearts. We must have faith in our truth and love for converting our opponents to our way. There is no doubt whatsoever that the deliverance of sixty million human beings from age-long suppression will not be brought about by mere showy demonstrations. There has to be solid and constructive programme contemplating an attack on all fronts. This enterprise requires concentrated energy of thousands of men, women, boys and girls who are actuated by the loftiest of religious motives. I would, therefore, respectfully urge those who don't appreciate the purely religious character of the movement to retire from it. Let those who have the faith and fervour, be they a few or many, work the movement.

The removal of untouchability may produce, indeed it will produce, great political consequences; but it is not a political movement. It is a movement purely and simply of the purification of Hinduism and that purification can only come through the purest instruments. Thanks be to God there are hundreds if not thousands of such instruments working in all parts of India. Let impatient sceptics watch, wait and see; but let them not mar the movement by hasty and ill-conceived interference even though it may be prompted by laudable motives.

—*The Bombay Chronicle*, 8-11-1932

5

Statement on Untouchability-IV

November 9, 1932

A correspondent writes as follows:[1] I consider your last fast to have been coercion of the worst type. I do not want to conceal from you my feeling about Yeravda Pact. I know my view is shared by public men who, because of their respect for your personality and because of your detention in the Yeravda Prison, did not like to say anything in public against your action in bringing about the Pact. I consider the Pact to be a public misfortune which would never have been brought about but for your unfortunate fast. I know of a very esteemed friend of yours who said that if the refusal had not meant your certain death he would never have given his consent to the Pact. There is a large number of thinking Hindus who regret having had to accept the Pact, as they think that there would have been no necessity for it if you had only accepted in London what you have done now.

In a statement you have said, "It was against these millions that my fast wass undertaken." I take it that was your intention but in actual result it was not these millions but others who had no course left open but to suspend their judgment and feeling in the matter and agree to terms to which nothing in the world would have made them agree, if their refusal had not meant losing your valued life. It was their spontaneous love that brought about the transformation inside of five days and brought into being the Yeravda Pact. If this is a correct statement of facts, will it not be more correct to say that it was only the fear of your death by starvation which brought about the Pact?

Remembering the circumstances under which it was brought about I think you will recognize that much need not be made of it; if the Pact is not carried out in its fullness, much less would there be any justification for you to embark on a second fast.

It gives me no pleasure to have to criticize a public man of your eminence, but the occasion is such that to keep quiet will not be quite honest.

Your assumption that the masses whom you have addressed on the question of untouchability have accepted your views on that question, simply because they did not publicly oppose your views, is not correct. Because of their respect for your great personality and because of your political leadership they would hear in silence and, however, much they may be opposed to your views, as I know many of them are, at least in Northern India, they would still consider it their duty to give you a respectful hearing. As you are aware, these people are not very vocal and they do not go out of their way to oppose the views of those who differ from them, and specially if the views are expressed by one of your eminence.

I have removed from the letter unnecessary paragraphs and names of public men referred to by the correspondent. It would be a matter of great grief to me if public men the correspondent mentions really suppressed their own opinions and accepted proposals which but for the threat of my death they would never have endorsed. If they acted as the correspondent suggests, they rendered a great disservice to the country and failed to appreciate the purely religious character of the fast. In public life one has often to perform the painful duty of sacrificing friends for the sake of truth or public weal.

And what was there in the Pact that these friends considered it to be highly objectionable? Surely not reservation of seats; not joint electorate, nor the method of nomination of candidates by primary election, as it has been called. They could not object to the resolution restoring to *Harijans* social and religious rights, of which they have cruelly remained dispossessed for ages. The only thing remaining is the number of seats allotted to them, but more than that was given to them by the Rajah-Moonje Pact, and as I have already said in a previous statement, caste Hindus could never give *Harijans* too many seats, if they really believed them to be their own kith and kin, whom they had hitherto kept under their heels. Sorry indeed is the outlook for them if what the Pact has given them is regarded as an undeserved concession wrung from reluctant caste Hindus by my fast.

Therefore, if the information given by my correspondent turns but to be true, I would hold my fast to be doubly justified. I should not care to live as a member of a society which is chary even of doing a small and tardy measure of justice to its outcastes, who are so through no fault of their own, and my fast was trebly justified if the further statement made by my correspondent is true that millions of whom I have been writing as a matter of fact never endorsed my vehement condemnation of untouchability and that they remained silent or even signified approval purely out of their respect for my "great personality" or my "political leadership". Life in the midst of such falsity would be a burden to me. The sooner public men and people realize the necessity of resisting and asserting themselves even against so called Mahatmas like myself, the better it would be for themselves, the country and for men like me. I should gladly fast even to have such a cleansing of the atmosphere.

My correspondent's is a timely contribution to the movement. Those who are in it should know the implications both of the movement and the prospective fast. I can only repeat with all the emphasis at my command that my fast is not intended to coerce anyone to act against what he may consider to be the best interests of society or country. My fast is not against persons whom I can name or number. It is intended imperceptibly and unconsciously to affect and agitate the millions whom I have in mind and between whom and me, I believe, an indissoluble bond exists. How such fasts work I do know from personal experience gained more than once.

My correspondent suggests that "there would have been no necessity for the Pact if I had only accepted in London what I have done now". I must not rake up the past beyond saying that I could not have done in London what it was possible to do in India. The correspondent although he was in London at the time simply does not know all the facts that are in my possession.

Let not the public, however, run away with the idea that I have many letters protesting against the Pact. So far as I can remember, this is the only letter of its kind. There are two or three letters complaining of coercion but none suggesting that, therefore, anything was given to *Harijans* that was not their due, and against this one letter I have hundreds of letters and telegrams warmly approving of the fast itself and the Pact. My closest associates both here and in the West with one or two exceptions have endorsed it and themselves felt its spiritual effect. But according to my wont and in order to keep the cause I espouse free from any harm, I publish letters containing hostile criticism, especially when it comes from men whom I know to be guided by friendly motives, as my correspondent undoubtedly is.

As I was handing in this statement, I received a wire from the ever-vigilant secretary of the All-India Anti-Untouchability League, pointing out that the total population of untouchables in India is not sixty millions but under forty. I am sorry for having given an incorrect figure, although Sjt. Thakkar corrected me even during the fast.

—*The Bombay Chronicle*, 10-11-1932

Note

1. The correspondent was Radhakant Malaviya; *vide* p. 380, and "Letter to C.Y. Chintamani", 11-11-1932.

6

Statement on Untouchability-V

November 14, 1932

In this fifth statement to the Press, in which I would like to express my gratefulness for the publicity they are giving to my statements and movement generally, I want to summarize a part of what I said last week to Sjt. Rajbhoj and his friends,[1] who met me to discuss practically the whole movement.

One of their questions related to what *Harijans* could do in order to help the movement. They could do a great deal in the direction.

They could anticipate the charges brought against them in justification of the refusal of some caste Hindus to associate with them on terms of absolute equality. I have already said in emphatic language that the caste Hindus are wholly to blame for the undoubtedly deplorable condition of the vast mass of *Harijans* and that the improvement will follow the removal of untouchability as a matter of course. It should never be made a condition of removal.

Nevertheless, it is the obvious duty of *Harijan* workers to carry on internal reform to the extent it is possible even in the face of the existing state of things.

Harijan workers should therefore devote all their energy to:

(1) The promotion of cleanliness and hygiene among *Harijans*.

(2) To improve the method of carrying on what are known as unclean occupations, such as scavenging and tanning.

(3) Giving up of carrion and beef, if not meat altogether.

(4) Giving up of intoxicating liquors.

(5) Onducing parents to send their children to day-schools wherever they are available and parents themselves to attend night schools wherever such are opened, and

(6) Abolition of untouchability among themselves.

Let me go through the items to indicate what is meant by them.

A daily bath is necessary at least in our climate, and clean clothes are necessary under all climates. I know that water is not easily available in Harijan quarters. They have, as a rule, no access to public wells and tanks, and they are too poor to afford a change of clothing. It is not generally realized that even a *lota*-full of water can give one a clean bath. It is taken by thoroughly wetting a clean towel and vigorously I rubbing the body, including the head, all over, and then wiping with a dry towel. If the bath is taken daily, the wet towel after wringing out all water from it can serve the purpose of drying the body. In this climate again, the same clothes can be easily washed and dried there and then, whilst one has merely the *langoti* on.

I know there is nothing new in what I am saying, and yet I have been obliged to explain these very elementary things to hundreds of workers. Even graduates have been found to be ignorant of these elementary aids to hygiene as to the improved method of scavenging.

Selfish, ignorant caste men make it well-nigh impossible to

remove human remains in a decent manner. The closets, because of the untouchability, are unclean beyond description. They are dark and illventilated and so constructed that only a portion is somewhat capable of being cleaned and that too under filthy conditions. To use these closets is a positive daily descent to Hell and but for the beneficent climate many more thousands than already do will find an early cremation. Owing to the superstitious refusal to see one's own faeces and to permit the untouchables or themselves to clean the interior of the closet, the *Harijans* who have to perform the very necessary social service can even in the existing unfavourable circumstances at least have their bath immediately after the cleaning is done and use plenty of dry earth for cleaning instead of just a little straw that they use.

Being an expert scavenger that I claim to be, I could show many very cheap, efficient and thoroughly clean methods of performing this service, especially if the villagers and city people would help, but I cannot deal with this interesting subject in this cursory statement. The curious may look up my writings on sanitation in general, and village sanitation in particular. Scavengers should wear a professional dress, while they are doing the cleaning work. Every employer or a group of employers can supply such a dress for his or their scavengers.

Clean tanning is a far more difficult proposition. Our tanners do not know the modern method of skinning carcases nor of tanning. Tanning I have here used in a comprehensive sense. The so-called higher classes having criminally neglected this useful body of their co-religionists and fellow-countrymen, the whole of the process from the carrying of the carcase to the dressing of the hide is done in a crude manner resulting in the loss to the country of untold wealth and the production of inferior hide.

The late Madhusudan Das,[2] who was a great philanthropist had himself learnt the modern process of tanning, had prepared statistics to show what the country was losing annually owing to the superstition of untouchability masquerading under the name of religion. Harijan workers can learn the modern method and acquaint the tanners with it in so far as it is practicable. The scavengers should be taught resolutely not to accept the remains of the householder's daily food which is virtually thrown at them in the cruellest manner possible. Years of habit have dulled the aesthetic sense of the scavengers and they see nothing wrong in eating the remains of another man's dishes. They crave for what they regard as dainties from their employers' dishes. I have known *Bhangis* having removed their children from school because the latter were taught not to touch these leavings and be satisfied with the *jowar* or the *bajri* bread baked in their homes.

Tanners should be induced to give up carrion and beef. As a vegetarian, I would like *Harijans* to give up, as many have done, meat altogether, but if they are not ready for this reform they should be taught to give up carrion as being unhygienic, besides being taboo by the rest of mankind and beef as being forbidden in Hinduism. I know that carrion is part of the price they get for removing the carcases. Dr. Ambedkar told me that in some places villagers beat those who had given up carrion, telling them it was their religion to eat it. The fact was that they were afraid that if the tanners gave up carrion-eating they would demand an equivalent price or give up carrying dead cattle. Whatever, the difficulty, carrion and beef eating must be given up. That one self-restraint will at once raise the *Harijans* in the estimation of the caste men and make the task of caste reformers comparatively easy in the campaign against untouchability.

Items four and five do not call for any remarks. They are self-explained.

The last item is abolition of untouchability among untouchables themselves. This is an urgent need. Removal of untouchability will become most difficult if this double untouchability is not removed with one sweep. It is an uphill task for Harijan reformers. But if they will realize that this movement is predominantly religious and is designed to purge Hinduism of the uncleanness that has crept into it, they will have the necessary courage and self-confidence to carry out the great reform.

It is needless for me to stress the point that workers in such a movement must be selfless and pure in character. I have given here a constructive programme, that should satisfy the most ambitious reformer among *Harijans* and occupy the whole of his time and energy. But there are one or two things he and the *Harijans* may not do during this period of grace. At any rate, no *Harijan* need fast against anyone nor need *Satyagraha* be offered by them. Let them watch the caste Hindus who are on their trial and see what they do to remove the bar that separates the *Harijans* from them. Let them not engage in quarrels with local caste-Hindus. Their behaviour should be at all times courteous and dignified, much more so at this time.

Religion can only be vindicated by self-suffering, never by violence done to the oppressors though there may be many things they may get by force. Their credit will lie in getting their rights by the conversion of caste Hindus and today they have ample reason for deriving hope from the knowledge that there are tens of thousands of caste Hindus who have a lively sense of their guilt and are straining every nerve to do reparation to *Harijans*. Let them have perfect confidence in the absolute justice of their cause and in the ability of self-suffering to win it.

In the next statement[3] I must give my reply to caste men who have asked what they can do to help the movement.

—*The Bombay Chronicle*, 15-11-1932

Notes

1. *Vide* "Interview to P.N. Rajbhoj", 11-11-1932.
2. In fact, Madhusudan Das was not dead. Gandhiji came to know of his mistake later from a member of the Ashram and at once apologized to Madhusudan Das. *Vide* Vol. LII, "Telegram to Madhusudan Das", 18-11-1932.
3. Vide "Statement of Untouchability-VI", 15-11-1932.

7

Statement on Untouchability-VI

November 15, 1932

If, among the *Harijans*, Sjt. Rajbhoj has yet been the only one to have asked me what *Harijans* might do to advance the movement, I have scores of letters from all parts of India, from caste Hindus, both men and women, students and others, inquiring in what way they can help without interfering with their other preoccupations; and since anti-untouchability is a movement, as applied to the masses, of merely change of heart and changing their attitude towards *Harijans*, the vast majority of the caste Hindus do not need to interrupt their daily activities in order to serve the *Harijans*.

The first thing is for everyone to understand the implications of the removal of untouchability in his or her own life, and if the answer is that he or she has not only no objection to, but is desirous of, seeing them entering public temples, using public places, such as schools, *serais*, roads, hospitals, dispensaries and the like, in short, to *Harijans* being put precisely on the same footing as themselves religiously, socially, economically and politically, he or she has personally taken the full step.

But that is not all that the questioners want or all that I should be satisfied with. Having gone so far, they want to know what more they can do in the furtherance of the cause. Such inquirers need not extend their activities beyond their immediate neighbourhood. Let them canvass the opinion of those with whom they come in daily contact, and if the former are not convinced of the necessity of removal of untouchability, they should, if they have critically studied the movement, endeavour to convince their neighbours or, if they are not competent, they should procure the necessary literature, supply them with it and put them in touch with those full-time workers who are specially qualified for such propaganda work. If they find that their neighbourhood is not touched by the spirit of the movement, and if they have any influence, they should arrange public lectures and demonstrations. So much for the work among caste Hindus.

But the real work that this large body of men and women can do is undoubtedly among the *Harijans*. Those caste Hindus who have studied my fifth statement could not fail to have noticed that there is a vast amount of silent and effective service to be rendered by caste Hindus without much expenditure of time, energy or money. Caste Hindus can effectively supplement the effort of *Harijan* workers in inculcating habits of cleanliness and by procuring facilities for having easy access to the required water supply. They can find out public wells and tanks situated near *Harijan* quarters and canvass the opinion of caste Hindus who may be using such wells or tanks, pointing out to them that *Harijans* have a legal right to the use of all such public services. And they can, at the same time, see to it that when the consent of caste Hindus has been secured for the use by *Harijans* of these services, the latter use them in a manner not offensive to the former.

As to scavenging, they can visit the owners of houses served by *Harijans* in their neighbourhood and explain to them the necessity of making it easy for *Harijans* to do the cleaning work in a hygienic manner. To this end, it would be naturally necessary for them to study the scientific method of constructing closets and disposing of nightsoil.

Thy can also procure from the householders special dresses to be supplied to the scavengers and make the *Harijans* feel by unhesitatingly doing the scavenging themselves that there is nothing low or undignified about rendering such service. Such workers should also carry on propaganda against caste men giving to their scavengers leavings from their daily food and, where they are ill-paid persuading the employers to pay them a decent wage.

As to tanning, not much help can be rendered, unless someone of such voluntary leisure-time workers has humanity and enthusiasm enough to study the hygienic method of skinning carcases and having done so, will spread the knowledge among tanners.

They certainly can do one thing. They can find out the custom about the disposal of such carcases and see that the tanners are assured of a proper wage for the service they rendered. Those who have capacity and time can conduct day or night schools, take Harijan children for picnics and sightseeing on holidays or whenever an opportunity occurs, visit *Harijans* in their own homes, procure medical aid where necessary and generally let them feel that a new page has been opened in their lives and that they need no longer regard themselves as the neglected and despised portion of Hindu humanity.

All that I have described can be most easily and efficiently done by the student world. If this work is done with silent zeal, determination and intelligence by a large body of men and women, I have no doubt that we shall have taken many steps in our progress towards the goal, and it would be found too that there are more things than I have described that require attention. I have but chosen a few of the many things that have come under my observation in the course of my journeyings.

—*The Bombay Chronicle*, 16-11-1932.

8

Statement on Untouchability[1]-VII

Poona, November 16, 1932

Though the questions that I shall endeavour to answer in this statement have been more or less covered by the previous statements, as they continue to recur, I thought it would be well to collect as many as possible and to deal with them in one single statement. "Are you not forcing people to do things against their will?" is one such question.

At least, such is not my intention.

The contemplated fast[2] is intended to stengthen the weak, to energize the sluggards and to give faith to the sceptics.

It should be clear to anyone who will give a little thought to it that those who are hostile to the reform will not only be unaffected by the fast, but will probably and perhaps rightly, from their own standpoint, welcome it, if only it ends fatally. An angry correspondent does not hesitate to say it in so many words, but says another correspondent, "it is all very well for you to say, you do not intend to do such and such a thing. There are many orthodox people who will follow the multitude for fear of personal injury from your over-zealous followers."

An argument like this can be advanced under almost any conceivable circumstance. I have led many movements in my lifetime where there has been no fast necessary, but the charge I am now answering has been brought against me often enough, in order to turn me away from my purpose.

Whatever, the intended consequences of the contemplated fast may be, apart from its being a question of honour, it must be taken up, if the occasion arises, for the additional reason that it is certain to stir to worthy effort tens of thousands of people who have faith in me.

Such must be the case in every movement of a religious character.

The second question is:

Are you not setting one section of the Hindus against another?

Most emphatically not. Some opposition is inevitable in every reform. But up to a point. Opposition and agitation in a society are a sign of healthy growth. I have no fear whatsoever of a permanent cleavage between the Sanatanists and the reformers. Far be it from me either to underrate the Sanatanist opposition or to disregard their sentiment.

I have no doubt whatsoever that some of them feel strongly that *Sanatan Dharma* is in danger. Nevertheless, it is astonishing how narrow at least in theory is the difference between the sanatanist and the reformer.

Almost every letter that I have received from the sanatanists makes these startling admissions:

1. We admit that there is much to be done for the amelioration of the condition of the *Harijans*;
2. We admit that many caste Hindus are ill-treating the *Harijans*;
3. We admit that their children should receive education and that they should have better quarters to live in;

4. We admit that they should have proper arrangement for bathing and drawing water for themselves;
5. We admit that they should have full political rights;
6. We admit that they should have ample facilities for worship; and
7. We admit that they should have all the civic rights that the others have.

But, say these sanatanists, "we must not be compelled to touch them or associate with them, especially whilst they are in their present condition."

Then I say to them, since you admit the necessity for putting them on the same level with you, why are you agitated that other caste Hindus will go a step further and believe on strength of the same *Shastras* that you believe in, that is, their duty is not to regard the *Harijans* as untouchables, but to have them share with themselves all those rights and privileges which you concede to them, but which you would have them to enjoy and exercise in isolation from you? Surely you who want to guard your own liberty of action and rightly resent the very idea of coercion, will not desire that the reformers should be coerced into carrying out schemes of amelioration which you hold to be necessary in exactly the same manner as you would like.

I venture to suggest a better way. Since you are at one with the reformers in conceding the desirability of ameliorating the condition of the *Harijans* and since you have not hitherto done anything tangible in that direction, subscribe liberally to the funds that the reformers are collecting, and use them as your agents for carrying out the common scheme and respect their interpretation of Hindu religion, as you would have them to respect yours. Hitherto, in practice, you have not resented the reformer's action in associating with the *Harijans*. You have suffered him to go his own way. You have not boycotted him. There is, then, no meaning in your opposition now simply because the movement has become more active and more universal than before.

One difficulty is still standing in the way. Who is to have the use of public temples and other public institutions that are in existence, and from which *Harijans* are at present debarred, in some cases legally and in other far more numerous cases, illegally? There is a very simple way out of the difficulty. If only each party will shed anger and mutual disrespect, a referendum can easily be taken for each village or a group of villages and each city or each division of a city, and whichever party has the majority in favour of its view should make use of the public institutions, including the temples. And if the sanatanists carry the majority with them, they should defray their share with the reformers of the cost of providing equal services for the reformers and the untouchables.

I bracket the reformers with the *Harijans*, for if they are worth their salt and will work up to their convictions, as time progresses, the duty must dawn upon them of denying to themselves the use of a single service which the *Harijans* cannot enjoy with the caste Hindus on absolutely equal terms.

Following out this train of reasoning the sanatanists will see that in justice they should bear the whole cost of bringing into being parallel services, because as I have understood the correspondence and as I have explained above, the sanatanists agree that the *Harijans* are entitled to the same services that they have hitherto enjoyed, and of which the *Harijans* have hitherto been deprived. Let not the sanatanists run away with themselves by picturing a condition of things as existing but which in reality does not exist.

Let them clearly understand that the removal of

untouchability in accordance with the Yeravda Pact[3], and with the declaration of the recently formed All-India Anti-Untouchability League includes no more than I have narrated. It does not include interdining and intermarriage.

That many Hindus including myself would go much further ought not to disturb the sanatanists. They will not want to stifle private judgment or private action, and if they have deep faith in what they believe, they should not take fright, in anticipation of what is to come.

If a particular reform has an inherent vitality and has come in response to the needs of the time, no power on earth can stem its irresistible march.

The third question is:

Are you not retarding political emancipation by forcing on public attention your views on social and religious questions, and springing upon the public a hurricane agitation for their acceptance?

I cannot answer this question at length without trespassing upon the limits which, as a prisoner, I have accepted for conducting the anti-untouchability campaign. But this much I can say that those who know me at all should understand that I draw no hard and fast line of demarcation between political, social, religious and other questions. I have always held that they are inter-dependent and that the solution of one brings nearer the solution of the rest. This does not exhaust the questions which I have collected from the correspondence which is already proving more than I can handle with the very limited assistance which only naturally I can have. I must deal with the rest to the best of my ability in the statement[4] to follow.

I would here like to urge the correspondents to be merciful.

Hitherto, I have punctiliously acknowledged almost all the letters that have reached me. But the correspondents will henceforth please be satisfied with whatever answers I can give through the series of statements I am issuing, and they will help themselves and me, if they will be brief and write only when they have something original to say or when they have questions to which they must have answers from me, before they can form their judgment on any issue arising in connection with the movement.

—*The Bombay Chronicle*, 17-11-1932

Notes

1. Issued by Gandhiji, from the Yeravda Central Prison, Poona. The earlier six statements were issued on the 4th, 5th, 7th, 9th, 14th and 15th November, 1932.
2. In sympathy with Kelappan's fast for the opening of the Guruvayur Temple to *Harijans*; *vide* "Statement on Untouchability–IX", 26-11-1932. The fast was to commence on January 2, 1933, but was postponed.
3. Between the leaders acting on behalf of the depressed classes and of the rest of the Hindu community, regarding the representation of the depressed classes in legislatures and certain other matters affecting their welfare. For the text of the agreement, *vide* Appendix "Agreement between depressed classes leaders and caste Hindu Leaders".
4. *Vide* "Statement on Untouchability—VIII", 17-11-1932.

9

Statement on Untouchability-VIII

Poona, November 17, 1932

Here is another question that many correspondents have asked:

> You say you believe in the *Shastras*. We do not understand what you mean by them, for you seem arbitrarily to reject many things which are supported by the *Shastras*. Even the *Gita* that you swear by requires one to follow the *Shastras*.

I must repeat what I have said in a previous statement[1] that for me, nothing that is inconsistent with the main theme of the *Gita* is *Shastra*, no matter where it is found printed. If I do not shock my orthodox friends, I would like to make my meaning clearer still.

Nothing that is inconsistent with the universally accepted first principles of morality has for me the authority of the *Shastras*. They are designed not to supersede, but to sustain the first principles, and the *Gita* is all-sufficing for me, because it not only conforms to the first principles, but gives you reasons for adherence to them at any cost.

But for this Golden Rule that I have suggested, laymen like me would flounder in the midst of a forest of conflicting texts and a pile of nicely printed and equally nicely bound Sanskrit volumes, for which rival pundits claim divine authority.

Thus, there are many *Smritis*, some of which are unknown outside the little areas in which, by a few hundred men they are held in veneration. No one can give their origin or the dates of their composition.

I saw one such volume in the South. When I inquired of the learned scholar friends about this volume, they told me that they had no knowledge of it.

There are numerous *Agamas*[2] which when examined, contradict one another and which have no binding effect outside the little areas where they find acceptance.

If all these books were to be held as binding on the Hindus, there is hardly an immoral practice for which it would be difficult to find Shastric sanction, and even in the hoary *Manusmriti* from which if the verses of doubtful authenticity are not expurgated, one would discover several texts contradicting the loftiest morals and teachings to be found spread throughout that great book. Therefore, the meaning I have given to the word '*Shastras*' in the *Bhagavad Gita*, wherein it occurs only in one context, is not any book or set of laws outside the *Gita* itself, but it means right conduct embodied in a living authority.

I know that this is not likely to satisfy the critic, and as a layman I can give no lead to anybody, but I can satisfy the curiosity of my critics by telling them what I mean exactly by the *Shastras*.

Another question put with equal persistence is this:

What do you mean by divine guidance or the inner voice, and how would you and for that matter the world, fare, if every one claimed such guidance for himself and each acted in a manner wholly different from his neighbours?

This is a fair question, and we would come to a pretty pass

if divinity had made no provision by way of self-protection. Whilst, therefore, all may lay the claim, some alone will be able to justify it. A person falsely claiming to act under divine inspiration or the promptings of the inner voice without having any such, will fare worse than the one falsely claiming to act under the authority of an earthly sovereign. Whereas the latter on being exposed will escape with injury to his body the former may perish body and soul together.

Charitable critics impute no fraud to me, but suggest that I am highly likely to be acting under some hallucination. The result for me, even then, will not be far different from what it would be, if I was laying a false claim. A humble seeker that I claim to be has need to be most cautious and to preserve the balance of mind. He has to reduce himself to zero before God will guide him. Let me not labour this point.

The claim I have made is neither extraordinary, nor exclusive.

God, will rule the lives of all those who will surrender themselves without reservation to Him. In the language of the *Gita*, God acts through those who have acquired complete detachment, i.e., self-effacement here.

There is no question of hallucination. I have stated a simple scientific truth, thus to be tested by all who have the will and the patience to acquire the necessary qualifications which are again incredibly simple to understand and easy enough to acquire where there is determination.

Lastly, no one need worry about my claim. What I am asking the people to do is capable of being verified by reason? Even when I disappear from the scene, untouchability will have to be removed.

Whether, the fast is divinely inspired or not, need not be a matter of concern even to my closest associates. They may, out of affection for me, work with double zeal in the cause. That would [not] be a calamity, even if it was found that the fast was the foolish act of a self-willed friend. Those who have neither affection for, nor faith in, me will remain unmoved by it. Constant harping, therefore, on the contemplated fast or my claim in regard thereto, is calculated to befog the public mind and the attention from the great work before the nation.

I would, therefore, conclude this statement by drawing the readers' attention to a few pictures that I have picked up from the voluminous correspondence in my possession.

Here is one from Vile Parle, suburb of Bombay (Now Mumbai), inhabited by well-to-do Hindus among others. The suburb has in round figures, 1,700 villas or houses; the Municipality has an income of Rs. 70,000 of which Rs. 31,000 are spent for conservancy. The scavengers are accommodated in quarters where there are no roads, no arrangement for water-supply and no sanitary convenience. The land itself is low-lying, the huts are hovels constructed from dilapidated tins which were once used for conservancy work. There is no lighting, and nearby is the dumping ground for all the suburban rubbish which gives an eternal stench.

Next to it is a structure for housing conservancy; attached to this is a water-pipe for washing dirty tins, and if the overseer is well disposed he would allow the scavengers to help themselves to water from the pipe; on the other side, is a row of carts that receive the buckets collected from the privies of households. It is in these surroundings that the scavengers have to pass their life. These quarters are surrounded by fields which are often under water, breeding mosquitoes, harbouring scorpions, snakes, field-rats. Thirty-one families live in this condition, they are composed of 35 men, 25 women, 34 boys and 15 girls.

Of this population of 109, only 9 boys can at all read and write with difficulty. The rest are utterly illiterate. This is a suburb where if the inhabitants, if they had any thought for these fellow-beings of theirs, could well afford to provide for them decent accommodation in decent quarters with lighting and water and other conveniences which are part of city life. There is work here for both the sanatanists and the reformers. It would be no answer to my complaint that the Vile Parle Municipality has an income of only Rs. 70,000 out of which it spends the princely sum of Rs. 31,000 on conservancy. I know that the inhabitants of Vile Parle are well-to-do enough to tax themselves specially on behalf of these useful servants of society. But I would regard that as a slow process. It is the primary duty of the Hindu habitants to make decent collections overnight and provide suitable quarters and other conveniences for the scavengers. If they did so, even then it would be a tardy performance of a simple duty done to fellowmen. When they have done this, there would be a point in their moving the Municipality to take up the burden of additional annual expenditure that would undoubtedly have to be incurred in order to enable the scavengers to live in comparative comfort.

An almost identical picture has been drawn by Sjt. A.V. Thakkar, the tireless Secretary of the All-India Anti-Untouchability League, of scavengers' quarters he has inspected during his travels undertaken on behalf of the League. He gives a harrowing tale about the condition of such quarters in Danapur and other places about Patna in Bihar. Now I wish that instead of engaging in fruitless controversy about what is not contained in the Shastras about untouchability, everyone of us would apply ourselves to ameliorating the conditions of the so-called untouchables. There is work enough and to spare for all my learned correspondents who almost without exception have assured me that they yield to no one in their desire to better their material and moral conditions.

—*The Bombay Chronicle*, 18-11-1932

Notes

1. *Vide* "Statement on Untouchability-I", 4-11-1932.
2. Scriptures.

10

Statement on Untouchability-IX

November 26, 1932

As January Ist is nearing, the correspondence on Guruvayur is increasing. Instead of answering one by one the questions that arise from the correspondence, it would perhaps be simpler to answer them by way of a mere statement of my position. The fast will begin on January 2 next if, before that date, the Guruvayur Temple is not opened to *Harijans* on the same terms as it is open to the caste Hindu sin general; but the fast will be postponed, if it becomes clear that the temple-going Hindus in the neighbourhood are opposed to the temple-entry of *Harijans* or if it is clear that although everybody is willing to open the temple to *Harijans*, there is a legal difficulty that cannot be overcome before Jannuary 2, next.

The majority of letters received by me assure me that the temple-goers are in favour of admission of Harijan worshippers to the temple. One or two correspondents vehemently contest the position and claim that a proper referendum will result in an overwhelming majority against such an entry. These correspondents have given me no proof in support of their opinion, whereas others say that they have actually taken referendum after their own fashion and found it to be in favour of temple-entry by *Harijans*. If the orthodox people will agree, a fresh referendum can at once be taken in the presence of referees appointed by both the parties. I need not repeat here the scheme suggested last Saturday in answer to a question from *The Times of India* correspondent. Anyway, the reform party should lose no time in fortifying their contention with incontestable proof.

They, however, say that, although the opinion of the templegoers may be overwhelmingly in their favour, the key of the temple is held by the Zamorin. That is no doubt technically true, but he is not the owner. He is a trustee representing the temple-going public.

Therefore, he cannot resist the clearly expressed wish of the majority of them. It is his duty to overcome the legal difficulties if there are any, and if he fails to do so, it simply means that the force of the public opinion has not become strong enough to compel the performance of his obvious duty.

The fast will then further solidify public opinion so as to make itself felt. The key to the temple, therefore, is in fact in the hands of the public. But as the legal maxim has it, law or equity helps the watchful, never the slothful. Let Kerala reformers, therefore, not blame the Zamorin.

It is discourteous and wrong to impute motives to him. If he refuses to open the temple to *Harijans*, let us think that he is not convinced of the public demand. His refusal must be a signal not for abusing him, but discovering the weakness in our position. It is surely more dignified and proper for the public to feel that it is a clearly expressed wish and cannot be flouted by its representative which the Zamorin is.

Guruvayur has already become an all-India concern. Let the caste Hindus all over India bestir themselves and declare their opinion that they desire Guruvayur Temple to be opened to *Harijans*. The moral force of such an opinion honestly and freely expressed will be irresistible.

I have already warned the reformers against using unbecoming language in respect of orthodox sanatanists or no-changers, as they have called themselves, in a petition addressed to H.E. the Viceroy.

They are entitled to their opinion. I look upon this untouchability question as primarily religious, and I would like both the no-changers and the reformers to work in a religious spirit without imputing motives to one another. No reform, much less religious reform, can be or should be carried by compulsion. I have repeatedly stated in unequivocal terms the limitations and functions of the proposed fast.

But a correspondent writing in Gujarati for himself and others says in effect:

It is all very well for you to say that you do not want to coerce anybody, but your position cannot but compel some people to act against their will. Some of us have no respect for your religious views or your social reforms, but we want you to live for your political power, and, therefore, if you persist in fasting, we will have to pocket our convictions and help you in your fight for temple-entry. If this is not coercion, we do not know the meaning of the word.

My answer is, I must not be expected to surrender my cherished convictions because I hold a prominent position in the Indian world, or because I have some political influence; I cannot barter away my faith or suppress its movement for the sake of retaining my social position or political influence. Everything is subservient to and is derivable from that faith. Ask me to deny or suppress it, and it would be worse than asking me to commit suicide. I would also venture to suggest that those who subordinate their convictions to their regard for my position or political influence can only have shallow convicions if any at all.

Convictions are made of sterner stuff. People have been known to stake their all for the sake of their convictions which may then be called religion.

The correspondent asks:

What is the poor Zamorin to do? On the one hand you and Mr. Kelappan will fast. On the other, 1,000 no-changers are said to have decided to do likewise. Whom is the Zamorin to please?

I answer without the slightest hesitation that he is to please neither party. He is there to please God, which is Truth. He is there to do his duty, and if it demands the sacrifice of thousands of no-changers, Mr. Kelappan and myself, he should have the courage to do so and he will deserve the honour of his own generation and posterity.

God will take care of the fasting fraternity. Those who fast will do so for defending the truth as they see it, and God of Truth will do what He likes with them. If their fast is in answer to an inner urge, it will be its own reward, and it will be well with them whether the purpose to which it is directed is apparently fulfilled or not.

The same correspondent persists:

But it is all very well for you to talk of the call of God, the conscience, the inner voice and all that. Others also can and do put forth the same claim. What are we, who have no inner voice and who have no God to parade before the public, to do and which are we to believe?

I can only say: You have to believe no one but yourselves. You must try to listen to the inner voice, but if you won't have the expression 'inner voice', you may use the expression 'dictates of reason' which you should obey, and if you will not parade God, I have no doubt you will parade something else which in the end will prove to be God for, fortunately, there is no one and nothing else but God in this universe. I would also submit that it is not everyone claiming to act on the urge of the inner voice who has that urge. After all like every other faculty this faculty for listening to the still, small voice within requires previous effort and training perhaps much greater than what is required for the acquisition of any other faculty, and even if out of thousands of claimants only a few succeed in establishing their claim, it is well worth running the risk of having and tolerating doubtful claimants.

So much for the Gujarati correspondent. I must now conclude this statement with a question from a correspondent who writes in English. His is a long letter containing elaborate argument but I think the following epitome correctly represents him:

> "Hitherto I have known you to be free from any trace of communalism but you now suddenly appear in a communal garb. I could have understood and justified your fast for swaraj or for all-India unity, but I cannot understand this fast on behalf of Hinduism. I have never taken you as a Hindu at all, certainly not as a narrow Hindu. What is there in opening the temples to *Harijans*, who do not want to go there"?

I am glad of this question. I have no desire whatsoever to appear to anyone as other than what I am. I am not ashamed of Hinduism or of the Hindu. I totally deny being narrow. I fancy I could not be held for one single moment by a narrow creed, and it is because the super-imposition of untouchability would make Hinduism a narrow creed that I have rebelled against it, and I would count my life to be a cheap price to pay for the removal of that blot.

I have nothing of the communalist in me, because my Hinduism is all-inclusive. It is not anti-Mussalman, anti-Christian or anti-any-other-religion. But it is pro-Mussalman, pro-Christian and pro-every-other-living faith in the world. To me, Hinduism is but one branch from the same parent trunk, whose roots and whose quality we judge only by the collective strength and quality of the different branches put together, and if I take care of the Hindu branch on whichI am sitting and which sustains me surely I am taking care also of the sister branches. If the Hindu branch is poisoned, the poison is likely to spread to others. If that branch withers, the parent will be the weaker for its withering.

If my correspondent and those who think with him have followed me hitherto, they will discover that if God gives me the privilege of dying for this Hinduism of my conception, I shall have sufficiently died for the unity of all and even for *Swaraj*. Finally let me repeat what I have said before now, that the question whether *Harijans* want to, or would enter into temples, if they were open to them, is irrelevant. The removal of untouchability is not a matter of bestowing patronage on *Harijans*. It is one of penance and purification by the caste Hindus and one of the penances they have to do is to open the Hindu temples and invite the *Harijans* to them.

—*The Bombay Chronicle*, 29-11-1932

11

Statement on Untouchability-X

December 9, 1932

One of the friends who attended the meeting of Anti-Untouchability League, which because of the prior body founded by Mr. V.R. Shinde bearing practically the same name will henceforth be called, and in my opinion more appropriately, the Servants of Untouchables Society, gave me a list of several questions with argument woven into them. For the sake of brevity, I reproduce the most important of these questions in the form of a letter:

As the Society has been formed at your instance and for the purpose of carrying out the programme for the removal of untouchability, workers naturally would expect your definite guidance. The first question that occurs to me then is this: Are the workers to constitute themselves as reformers, doing[1] Addressee's wife work of uplifting untouchables or uplifting themselves and if it is to be the latter, should not the greatest stress be laid upon work amongst caste Hindus themselves, and if so how is that work to be done?

This is a comprehensive question and in answering it, I hope to be able to cover the main points raised by my friend. I have repeatedly declared in unequivocal terms that caste Hindus are sinners who have sinned against those who are called untouchables. Caste Hindus are responsible for the present condition of the untouchables. Immediately, therefore, they repent for the sin and purify themselves by removing the load of untouchability from off the backs of untouchables, we shall discover perfect transformation among the latter. Not that they will at once shed the habits of a lifetime, but there would be conscious effort on their part to shed those habits and everywhere the multitude of caste Hindus will be helping them to give up those habits.

It would be like the suppressed members of a family rejoining the suppressors, feeling the warmth of reunion and suppressors receiving them as if they were never separated. I am painfully conscious of the fact that such a consummation will take some time before it comes, but it will never come unless some of us understand and adopt the right attitude. Even among the liberal-minded workers, I have often heard the opinion expressed that untouchability should be removed only when the *Harijans* give up their bad habits, educate themselves and live clean lives utterly forgetting that *Harijans* cannot do these things whilst they remain untouchables. Even if they would, they forget also that individual *Harijans* who are living decently are not received on terms of equality by caste Hindus and the very best amongst them are denied the ordinary amenities of life every day and contact with caste Hindus. Their birth constitutes the automatic cause for the penal servitude for life which cannot be commuted by any change in manners or any other consideration. Hence, there is and can be no incentive to better their mode of life. The idea has taken deep root in their minds that they may hope for no redemption at least during their present lifetime.

The only way therefore, is to undo the mischief and make them realize the dignity of their status as men. Caste Hindus should first unconditionally take them up as their very own and then and then only can a change in their condition on a vast scale take place. Therefore, the first and foremost items in the programme of work should be a whirlwind propaganda for educating and canvassing opinion among caste Hindus. This work can be done by personal visits on a most intensive scale and by flooding the country with literature on the subject.

In my opinion untouchability is as self-demonstrated a sin as untruth. The proposition does not need the support of *Shastras*. Nevertheless, as there is a body of learned men who invoke the aid of *Shastras* in order to justify untouchability by reason of mere birth, it would be well for workers to arm themselves with pro-reform literature. There is a growing body of learned men in *Shastras* who emphatically hold that untouchability as it is believed and practised today, has no support whatsoever in the *Shastras*.

This propaganda can only be entrusted to workers who have character to lose, those who will not be easily ruffled by insults, who have patience to listen to counter argument and wit enough to combat it. In a movement of religious reform, there is no room whatsoever for coercion in any shape or form. Reformers will have to submit to their fate if as a result of this personal canvassing it is discovered that a vast majority of Hindus have no sense of sin about untouchability or even otherwise are averse to its removal and the consequent raising of the *Harijans'* status. They will have then without being irritated against the majority shown by personal suffering that they are in the right and the majority in the wrong and this they can best do by making common cause with *Harijans* and voluntarily denying themselves those rights and conveniences which are today denied to *Harijans*.

Such an act of self-denial by a large body of men and women will by itself fill the *Harijans* with hope and raise them in their own estimation and encourage them to an effort for self-improvement. The most effective work that can be done among caste men is to induce them to take one Harijan at least per family either as member or at least as domestic servant. There is an ancient practice in well-to-do households never to take their meal without having at least one guest to share it with them. Now-a-days, this is more observed in the breach than in the performance. This act is described as one of the five daily *Yajnas* or sacrifices. I cannot conceive of a better mode of offering this yajna than that of having a Harijan to share the meal with us.

This must not be confused with interdining. For me, interdining means dining with those who may touch your food and whose food you may touch but dining together under the same roof without the mutual touch does not mean interdining.

If untouchability of *Harijans* is removed, there can be no objection to their sharing the family meal precisely on the same terms as other castes. There are again innumerable social functions and ceremonies to which *Harijans* are never invited by caste men. Their cattle and other domestic animals may share their joys and sorrows but not *Harijans* or, if they do, these are occasions when they are pointedly reminded that they are not the same sort of human beings as caste Hindus.

I have pointed out only a few illustrations of the kind of propaganda and work that can be and should be done amongst caste men to purge themselves of the sin but, even as special treatment and care are bestowed upon a banished member of the family when he is recalled, so will caste men do the work amongst *Harijans* themselves when the sense of sin has really dawned upon them. They will then go to the *Harijans* not as teachers or donors but as debtors going to their creditors to discharge their obligations and in that humble spirit they will offer to teach them, their children and otherwise help them in every way possible for them.

It has been suggested that if this constructive programme is taken up, it would prove too expensive and too long-drawn-out to be of immediate service, and to do it would be a programme by itself on the part of a handful of reformers. It assumes a different shape when it is conceived as an item in the programme of self-purification. A tree is judged by its fruit and so has the changed spirit of caste men to be judged by its results. It is, therefore, not enough for them to be able to say that they have touched half a dozen *Harijans* during the day or even that they have fed a Harijan but their newly born affection for them should make them impatient to render this neglected portion of humanity every help that it is in their power to render.

After all, *Harijans* themselves have to feel the effect of the new awakening in Hinduism and they cannot do so unless caste men come in contact with them in every walk of life and every activity. If the awakening is universal, constructive programme will not prove expensive.

Local volunteers will work in their own localities without needing any payment and if the awakening is not universal it becomes the double duty of workers to tackle the constructive programme.

Therefore, whether it is slow or quick, expensive or inexpensive, I have no doubt it must be the integral part of the activities of the society. It may not be able to overtake all Harijan children, or all Harijan sick needing medical aid but whatever is done in that direction will count and should be an earnest of more to come.

Moreover, the monetary contributions will be the index of the extent to which caste Hindus have responded to the call of the age. In this programme temple-entry occupies the most important place, for, when the innumerable public temples are opened to *Harijans* they will immediately feel the dawning of a new era for them. They will forget that they were once the outcastes of the society. Intermingling at temples will of itself induce a change in their outlook and in their lives. They will forsake their objectionable habits. But say some of my correspondents:

> "What are temples worth today? They are dens of iniquities. All kinds of practices are going on there."

I have a cutting before me containing a letter from a lady drawing an ugly picture of what is going on in a famous temple. I do not know how far charges made against some of these celebrated shrines are true. There is no doubt that temples are not what they must have been when they were built. Temple-reform in itself is a separate subject. Their deterioration cannot be pleaded as valid reason for not opening them to *Harijans* and I know that vast mass of poor people who visit these temples are untouched by corruption that may be going on in them; and whatever may be true of famous temples is undoubtedly not true of village temples. Village temples were and even now are a place of refuge for villagers. It is difficult to conceive the life of a Hindu villager being regulated without his temple. Whether it is birth or death or marriage in a Hindu family, temple plays a prominent part.

Therefore, *Harijans* must have access to it. But says another correspondent:

> "If you do not insist on *Harijans* conforming to certain regulations such as cleanliness, you will lower the already tottering reputation of temples."

I anticipate no such catastrophe. What I have said is that no special condition should be laid down for the entry of *Harijans* that is not applicable to every other Hindu worshipper.

I heartily endorse that suggestion of Dr. Bhagwandas that instead of untouchability senselessly attaching to birth, it should attach to individual's outward conduct.[1] One cannot regulate inward cleanliness but it is possible to regulate outward conduct and, therefore, those whose habits are unclean, who are unwashed and unkempt, who are drunk, should be regarded untouchables till they have cleaned themselves even as every human being all the world over in decent society is untouchable whilst he is in a dirty condition from any cause whatsoever. But under the cover of specious argument as cleanliness, etc., *Harijans* should no longer be kept without payment of the debt due to them by caste men.

The first step, therefore, is to receive them as they are, subject only to general regulations, not specially imposed for the occasion, but the regulations that have been in vogue before reforms came. New regulations may undoubtedly be framed after freedom of *Harijans* is honestly declared and assured to them.

—*The Bombay Chronicle*, 10-12-1932

Note

1. *Vide* also "Letter to Bhagwandas" 14-12-1939.

12

Statement on Untouchability-XI

December 14, 1932

Supposing on the strength of your statement[1] that in the event of the Referendum going against you, you would have to postpone your fast indefinitely, voters, although they may be in favour of *Harijans* entering the Guruvayur Temple, give their votes against you for the sake of preventing the fast, what would you do?

This is a question asked of me. I should hope there would be no such trickery resorted to by the voters. If, however, it is discovered that they have resorted to any such trickery, I can only say that they would be endangering my life more than if they voted honestly and according to their convictions.

Having put my life at stake for the removal of untouchability, I hope I shall not be found so cowardly as to save it by taking advantage of any dodge. What I have said about the postponement refers only to honest voting.

If I am satisfied that the majority of temple-goers in the neighbourhood of Guruvayur are really against temple-entry by *Harijans*, and if I still persisted in fasting, I should be guilty of using coercive measures in order to secure my end. I am not conscious of ever having done such a thing in my life, and I am not likely to do so now, when I may be nearing my end, to deny the practice of a lifetime. I am most anxious to preserve the approaching fast against the slightest taint of coercion, and I have no doubt that at the end of it, it would be found to have been free from reproach. I am watching, as a scientist would watch, the effect the contemplated fast is producing, and it fills me with hope and delight. It has set the people thinking, and it will certainly not compel any person to act against his conscience; but it is making sluggish people shed their sluggishness and act promptly, that is to say, that it is moving to action those who bear affection towards me.

I am not sorry for that movement. Those who think that I am attempting to corrupt Hinduism, write to me angry letters and invite me to anticipate the fast and thus hasten my death. I do not mind such letters. I am used to receiving them. I merely refer to them to show that those who are opposed to the removal of untouchability are not likely to be affected by any fast that I may embark upon; and much less by the mere contemplation of it, and this is as it should be. I should like to say more about the origin of the fasting method under the given circumstances in my life. I must, however, postpone this to a future date. At the moment, I can only say that neither Srijut Kelappan nor I can be deterred from the step which has been dictated to us by our consciences.

When every effort is being made to ensure the honesty of the Referendum, it comes as a painful surprise to me that the Zamorin is making charges of fraud against those who are engaged in the Referendum work. I regard him as an honourable man. He knows that Srijut Madhavan Nair, who is the chairman of the Referendum Committee, is a well-known advocate respected throughout Kerala, and is assisted by Srijut Rajagopalachari, who is on the spot. I do not know of any of the leading workers who would tolerate any questionable practice.

It is, therefore, the duty of the Zamorin or any other person who may hear anything about the fraudulent practice, to bring it to the notice of the Committee. It is impossible to deal with the general charge unsupported by any evidence. There is no occasion to import passion or partisan feelings into what is purely a moral and religious question; but the orthodox party and the reformers can, if they will, work in close association for the elucidation of truth. I can only repeat my assurance so often given by me that if I found I was wrong about the local public opinion being in favour of temple-entry, I should immediately retrace my step. I have no other end to serve but that of truth.

—*The Bombay Chronicle,* 15-12-1932

Note

1. *Vide* "Letter to P.N. Rajbhoj", 8-12-1932.

13

Statement on Untouchability-XII

December 15, 1932

I thought I had made my position quite clear about the limitations of the temple-entry agitation. But I see sanatanist friends are still agitated over a fancied danger which they think *Sanatan Dharma* is facing from this agitation. I, therefore, summarize below what I have said in published statements and letters to correspondents:

1. The method of fasting is at the present moment confined only to Guruvayur. There are historic reasons for the fast from a reformer's standpoint. There was no escape from it. Those reasons I know will not be accepted as any justification by the opponents of reform or even by all who believe in temple-entry. My purpose in referring to it is merely to state the limitations of the fast.
2. The fast as contemplated will not be undertaken if the referendum goes against the reformers. It will be postponed if it is found that the existing law is against reformers and that every effort is made for the necessary legislation and Viceregal sanction has been obtained for the introduction of a Permissive Bill, that the Bill cannot go through the Legislature before 2nd January, 1933.

3. I would not be a party to any forcible temple-entry in defiance of the wishes of a majority of worshippers at the respective temples and the agitation will be confined only to public temples. Therefore, the opening of private temples will depend entirely upon their owners and the restrictions applicable to caste Hindus will naturally be applicable to *Harijans.*

In my opinion, these limitations ought to satisfy any reasonable Hindu, but I know there is a body of opinion which will not tolerate the opening of any existing Hindu temple to *Harijans* on the same terms as to other Hindus. For such uncompromising opponents, there is no method of conciliation that I can devise short of a programme of new temple building. That means a sharp additional division in an already divided society, but I am convinced if the reformers will loyally and honestly abide by the limitations I have suggested, the unreasonable opposition will die for want of support. Those who have arrogated to themselves the name *Sanatan Dharma,* should not be surprised or shocked if opponents also derive authority for reform from the same scriptures that the sanatanists profess to believe in. There is a growing body of *Shastris,* well versed in Sanskrit lore, who believe that it is not only permissible in Hinduism to admit 'untouchables' to public temples, but that it is wrong to prohibit them from offering worship in common with other Hindus at these temples. These pundits also believe that there is no such thing as untouchability, attaching to birth and incapable of being cured by any penance or purification.

They do believe in untouchability attaching to acts and occupations, but this is no peculiarity to Hinduism. It is common to all religions and is based upon sound hygienic principles.

I believe, too, that the alarm caused over the proposed legislation is also based on ignorance. So far as I understand the proposal, it simply amounts to this. If a two-thirds majority of worshippers at a particular temple express their desire through a regular channel devised by the legislature, such temples should be thrown open to *Harijans* on terms of equality with others. In my opinion, the proposal itself is so intrinsically sound that no reasonable person can have anything to say in opposition to it.

Anyway, let the opponents of reform understand exactly what the reformers seek to achieve. As it is, I am sorry to have to observe an agitation against reform being conducted in disregard of facts and that it is being sustained by statements that are contrary to truth and by baseless insinuations and imputations. Such methods can do no harm to reform if it is sound in itself, but it hurts Hinduism if the reformers or their opponents resort to methods that are less than fair and just.

—*The Hindu*, 16-12-1932

14

Statement on Untouchability-XIII

December 30, 1932

I had full consultation with Mr. C. Rajagopalachari, Mr. K. Madhavan Nair and Mr. Kelappan[1], who have come to Poona to confer with me. They have placed the results of the Guruvayur referendum before me. The referendum was taken of the Ponnani Taluk where the temple is situated.

Never perhaps was a referendum taken with such scrupulous care or with such scientific precision before this. Rarely to my knowledge, have 73 per cent of the eligible voters voted.

In order to find out the truth, voting was confined only to those who were actual temple-goers, that is to say, those who were not entitled to enter the Guruvayur Temple and those who would not, such as the Arya Samajists, were excluded from the voters' list. I had intended without thinking of all implications actually to find out by some method of examination, who were actual temple-goers, but I have found it to be utterly impracticable. It was enough to announce that only those should vote who believed in temple-going, who had faith in temple-worship as an integral part of the Hindu religion and who were entitled to enter the Guruvayur Temple.

The total population entitled to the temple-entry being approximately 65,000, the outside estimate of adults may be taken as 30,000. As a matter of fact, 27,465 adult men and women were actually visited for receiving their votes. Of these 55 per cent were in favour of temple-entry; nine per cent against, eight per cent were neutrals, and 27 per cent abstained.

It should be remembered that the referendum was taken amidst adverse influences. The Zamorin would not co-operate, and I am sorry to have to say, even cast aspersions upon the workers and the procedure they followed. The Ponnani Taluk is the stronghold of orthodoxy and yet there was a decisive majority in favour of admission of the untouchables to that shrine now made famous throughout the length and breadth of the land.

The figures were also instructive, as showing that both men and women had no hesitation in spite of the contemplated fast, of expressing their dissent. I would also draw a fair deduction from the neutrals and non-co-operators. They could not at all, if they had chosen to give their decision, be regarded as against the temple-entry of the *Harijans*. It would not be a bad or unfair guess to make, if I suggested that a fourth of these, at least, were probably for temple-entry. The percentage of the voters favouring temple-entry would then be sixty-five per cent of the total eligible voters. If they be excluded altogether from the referendum, the majority would be 77 per cent.

Turn the figures as we may, the unchallengeable conclusion is that a decisive majority of eligible voters are in favour of the entry by the *Harijans*.

That fact shows that Mr. Kelappan's statement that the majority of temple-going population surrounding Guruvayur was in favour of temple-entry, is correct.

In view of the official announcement that the Viceregal decision as to the sanction for the introduction in the Madras Legislative Council of Dr. Subbaroyan's permissive Bill with reference to the temple-entry could not possibly be announced before the 15th of January, the fast contemplated to take place on the 2nd day of the New Year will be indefinitely postponed, and in any case up to the date of the announcement of the Viceregal decision. Srijut. Kelappan concurs with this postponement. As the contemplated fast was addressed to the public, let me, at the risk of repeating what I have said previously, state my own position clearly. My fast, I regard, as a purely spiritual act, and therefore not capable of being fully explained.

But in so far as I can, I may say that it is intended to stir the public conscience. Hinduism teaches that when evils and corruption are beyond control by ordinary means and, human endeavour is supplemented by *tapasya* or penance which, in its extreme form, means fasting either conditional or unconditional.

Therefore, it is no new thing. But for the influence, supposed or real, I enjoy among the masses, perhaps no notice would be taken of it.

My conviction is that Hinduism has fallen from the purity and vitality it once had. Its very scriptures are evidence of the continuous progress and adaptability to circumstances that arose from time to time. Though it has retained unimpaired the claim to divine inspiration for the scriptures as a body, it did not hesitate to introduce new reforms and make changes. Hence, it is that we have in Hinduism not only Vedas, but all later writings claiming authority. But a time came, when this healthy growth or evolution was arrested, and instead of the written word being used as an aid to the search for light from within, it was held to be all-sufficing, whether it accorded with longings and strivings of the spirit within or not. The descendants of those who wrestled with God Himself and drew from Him some of the imperishable things one finds in Vedas and later writings, felt too exhausted for further effort, either to wring out new meaning from an old verse or *mantra* or produce a new *mantra*. They felt that they had done with God and that God had finished His work, after inspiring the last verse of the latest Shastra. And so one finds an army of interpreters seeking to reconcile, often irreconcilable texts, unmindful as to whether they answer the pressing needs of the age or whether they can stand the light of searching examination. And even penances took mere outward form, instead of being an expression of the inward agonizing struggle. I may be wrong in my diagnosis, but such being my case and finding the Hindu society irresponsive to the central call of Hinduism, that is, progressive realization of unity of all life, not as a philosophical doctrine but as a solid fact of life, I thought that by continuous effort to live my religion as I understood it, I had the fitness for doing penance by way of fasting and that I had such a call from within.

I hope it is easy for the reader to see that there is no coercion behind the fast thus conceived. If my fast was fixed as an unconditional one, it is obvious there can be no coercion about it, for nothing that the public may do or not do could suspend my fast. Therefore, if a conditional fast is held to be coercive, it would be so considered because of the condition. My experience is that the fast has not deterred people from sticking to their principles or even their inclinations, as was seen at Guruvayur.

The public will now understand that the postponement is what it means and no more. The fast was intended to secure admission of the untouchables into the Guruvayur Temple, and if its resumption is necessary in a legitimate manner to secure the opening, it will certainly come, as for instance, if through the mere supineness of the reformers and consequent want of expression by public opinion in demanding the necessary legislation to remove the block created by decisions of courts and the Law of Trusts or the Madras Religious Endowments Act, which itself was a measure affecting religion, naturally the fast has to be resumed.

That is to say, it must be resumed, if the original vow is to be fulfilled. The fast must be resumed for the acts of omission or commission by those who are believed to be in favour of opening the Guruvayur Temple.

The Yeravda Pact was entered into between the representatives of the caste Hindus and the *Harijans*, and while confirming the Pact at the memorable conference in Bombay, the former resolved as follows:

> "This conference resolves that henceforth, amongst Hindus, no one shall be regarded as untouchable by reason of his birth and that those who have been so regarded hitherto, shall have the same rights as the other Hindus in regard to the use of public wells, public schools, public roads and other public institutions. These rights shall have statutory recognition at the first opportunity, and shall be one of the earliest Acts of the Swaraj Parliament, if they shall not have received such recognition before that time. It is further agreed that it shall be the duty of all Hindu leaders to secure, by every legitimate and peaceful means, an early removal of all social disabilities now imposed by caste Hindus upon the so-called untouchable classes, including bar in the respect of admission to temples."[2]

If the distinguished caste Hindus that passed the resolution, represented, as they claim to, the Hindu portion of the Indian Nation, the claim has to be made good by increasing fraternization day by day with *Harijans* on the part of caste Hindus by way of opening to them public institutions.

Mr. Kelappan's fast over the opening of the Guruvayur Temple was actually going on whilst the Pact was emerging, and I asked him to suspend it principally at the suggestion of the Zamorin of Calicut.

Moreover, as I have already said, when on the British Government's acceptance of relevant portion of the Pact I broke the fast, I solemnly assured Dr. Ambedkar and took a vow in the secret of my heart and in the presence of God that I would hold myself as a hostage for the fulfilment of the resolution above mentioned, and the general carrying out of the Pact by the caste Hindus. It would be a betrayal of trust and a betrayal of the *Harijans* if, in any shape or form, I slackened my effort or gave up altogether the intention of fasting in connection with the removal of untouchability.

I would like the voiceless and helpless *Harijans* to feel that thousands of Hindu reformers, as zealous of Hindu religion and scriptures on which it is based, as any Hindu calling himself a sanatanist can be, are prepared, no less than I am, to sacrifice their lives, if need be, in an attempt to remove untouchability, root and branch.

There can be no rest, therefore, for me or those who, by word of mouth or show of hands, silently endorsed the resolution, until untouchabilty becomes a thing of the past It would be only out of the ashes of untouchability that Hinduism can revive, and thus be purified and become a vital and vitalizing force in the world.

—*The Bombay Chronicle*, 31-12-1932; also
The Hindu, 31-12-1932

Notes

1. *Vide* Appendix "Discussion with K. Kelappan", 29-12-1932.
2. This resolution was drafted by Gandhiji and passed by the conference with Malaviyaji in the chair on September 25, 1932; *vide* "Resolution at the Hindu Leaders' Conference, Bombay", 25-9-1932, where, however, "imposed by custom" is found instead of "imposed by caste Hindus".

15

Statement on Untouchability in Hindu Shastras

January 3, 1933

I have had the privilege, as the public knows, of having a friendly discussion with Bhagwan Shastri Dharurkar of Pandharpur and others who accompanied him. These gentlemen came, as they made it clear to me, in their personal capacity, and not as representatives of any association. They came with a view to understanding my position regarding untouchability in general and the movement for temple-entry by *Harijans* in particular. No doubt they had also the intention of helping me to understand and even adopt the *Sanatani* viewpoint, for which they were speaking.

I had a long discussion with them. In order to leave no stone unturned in my attempt to understand the viewpoint of *Sanatani* pundits and in accordance with the arrangement made with Bhagwan Shastri Dharurkar, I had invited some friends, learned in the Shastras and who, I knew, generally supported my position, so that I may have both the schools of thought playing upon my mind.

I can say that I listened to their arguments and discourses with the greatest patience and with respectful attention. I was unable to find any error in the position which I have held for a period now nearing half-a-century. I know that time never runs in favour of an error, and as I regard myself as a humble seeker after truth and prone to error like any other mortal, I have always held myself ready to confess errors as soon as the conviction went home; but these discussions have left me more convinced than ever that untouchability, as it is practised today in Hinduism, has no warrant in the Hindu Shastras.

Many have done me and themselves great injustice by not giving their full value to the expression "as it is understood and practised today". But rather than just state the effect produced on my mind by these prolonged discussions, I have secured from the pundits or *Shastris* who gave me general support, their interpretation of the *Shastras* about untouchability, and I have pleasure in giving below an authorized translation of the statement which is in Hindi. Acharya Anandshankar Dhruva and Dr. Bhagwandas are responsible for this translation.

The statement runs as follows:

Three kinds of untouchables are mentioned in the Hindu *Dharmashastras*:

(1) Persons classed as untouchables by birth, i.e., progeny of the union of a Shudra with a Brahmin woman.

(2) Persons guilty of any of the five heinous sins or of certain practices condemned in Hinduism, and

(3) Persons whilst they are in a polluted state.

There is nothing to show that any of the communities now classed as untouchables come under the first category. Therefore, the rules governing untouchability and ex-communication under the first head are inapplicable to them. Assuming that any of these communities can be brought under the first head, they can be free from their untouchability and have all the privileges enjoyed in common by the four *varnas* by clean living, initiation into the Shaiva or Vaishnava worship, and the like.

The second kind of untouchability obviously cannot attach exclusively to any class or community as a whole. It may apply to individuals in any and every community. The untouchability of the untouchables so-called, is not due to their fallen state under the second head, nor can they be shown to be descendants of such fallen parents. Persons guilty of heinous sins, referred to under the second head, become fully purified by the performance of appropriate purificatory ceremonies. The progeny of such fallen persons as have not become thus purified cannot be classed as untouchables. Some *Smritikaras* who regard such progeny as untouchables, prescribe a very slight purificatory ceremonial for their restoration; and persons who are guilty of practices rendering them untouchable can also be free from untouchability by giving up such practices.

The third kind of untouchability, due to one's being in a polluted state, obtains among all classes whether regarded as untouchables or not. There is nowarrant in the *Shastras* for considering tanners, *Bhangis* and others as permanent untouchables, merely by reason of their occupation. Their untouchability is due to the external uncleanness caused by the nature of their work. All untouchability under the third head is cured by a bath and a change of clean clothes at the due time.

Thus, it is necessary that the rights common to four *varnas*, e.g., of entry into temples, educational institutions, of use of public wells, ghats, tanks, rivers, etc., should equally accrue to the untouchables so called, and that it is wrong to deprive them of such common rights. This is probable from the texts, the fundamental principles and the spirit of the *Dharmashastras*.

- Swami Kevalanand

- Narayan Shastri Marathe
- Laxman Shastri Joshi
- Bhagwandas
- Anandshankar Dhruva
- Indiraraman Sastri
- Keshav Laxman Daftari
- P.H. Purandare

I do not need to introduce the signatories to the public, but I can say that they claim to Sjt. C.V. Vaidya. All these I hope to share with the public as early represent *Sanatan Dharma* no less than those who call themselves sanatanists. Apart from these, I have received valuable opinions in general support from Mahamahopadhyaya Pramathanath Tarkabhushan, Pundit Shreedhar Shastri Pathak, Krishna Thanasukh Misra and last but not the least as it is possible to have them printed simultaneously with this. I am issuing to the Press the original Hindi and authorized translations in Marathi and Gujarati, and I hope that the respective journals would only print the authorized text.

The opinion of these learned men, popularly construed, means that no class of persons today bears the brand of permanent untouchability. It is obvious that untouchability by birth cannot exist today in connection with a class. In connection with individuals, it is practically impossible of detection. There are undoubtedly men who must be guilty of the five heinous sins, but all castes are capable of committing those sins, and society today takes no notice of them. The condemned practice under the second head refers to eating of carrion or beef. There are undoubtedly some people among those classed as untouchables who are given to this practice, but they are bound to give it up as soon as caste Hindus make the real advance. At the present moment the very incentive to give up beef or carrion is lacking. The temporary pollution under the third head carries no condemnation with it. It is a pollution which is inevitable for all in a certain state, and the pollution ceases immediately the state ceases.

If the signatories have correctly interpreted by the *Shastras*, then we have been all these many years doing a grave injustice to *Bhangis*, tanners and others by classing them as permanent untouchables, although we recognize that their profession is as honourable as any and much more indispensable for the very existence of society than many others which do not carry the mark of untouchability with them.

—*M.K. Gandhi*[1]

Note

1. *The Hindu,* 4-1-1933.

16

Why 'Harijan'

Several correspondents have asked me why I have adopted the name '*Harijan*' for 'untouchable'. Some English friends have asked me for its meaning. It is not a name of my coining. Some years ago, several 'untouchable, correspondents complained that I used the word *asprishya* in the pages cf *Navajivan*[1]. *Asprishya* means literally untouchable. I then invited them to suggest a better name and one of the 'untouchable' correspondents suggested the adoption of the name 'Harijan', on the strength of its having been used by the first known poet-saint of Gujarat. Though the quotation he sent me did not exactly fit the case he wanted to make out for the adoption, I thought that it was a good word. '*Harijan*' means 'a man of God'. All the religions of the world described God pre-eminently as the Friend of the friendless, Help of the helpless and Protector of the weak. The rest of the world apart, in India who can be more friendless, helpless or weaker than the forty million or more Hindus of India who are classified as untouchables? If, therefore, any body of people can be fitly described as men of God, they are surely these helpless, friendless and despised people. Hence, in the pages of *Navajivan*, since the correspondence, I have always adopted *Harijan* as the name signifying untouchables. And, when God chose to entrust me with their service even whilst undergoing imprisonment, I could not use any other word for describing them. I recoil with horror from that word and all it implies. Not that the change of name brings about any change of status, but one may at least be spared the use of a term which is itself one of reproach. When caste Hindus have of their own inner conviction and, therefore, voluntarily got rid of the present-day untouchability, we shall all be called *Harijans*, for, according to my humble opinion, caste Hindus will then have found favour with God and may, therefore, be fitly described as His men.

—*M.K. Gandhi*[1]

Note

1. *Vide* "My Notes", *Harijana.*

APPENDICES

Appendix-1

Discussion with B.R. Ambedkar

September 22, 1932

AMBEDKAR: We must accept that in the country there are two groups belonging to two different ideologies and act accordingly, and I should get my compensation. I also want that a clear understanding should be arrived at which would recompense me in other respects also. The decision of the Government gives me seventy-one seats and I feel that is a just, reasonable and definite allocation.

GANDHIJI: According to you.

A. Over and above that I get the right to vote and contest elections in the general constituencies. I also have a franchise in the labourers'constituencies. We do realize that you are of immense help to us.

G. Not to you personally.

A. But I have only one quarrel with you, that is, you work for the so-called national welfare and not for our interests alone. If you devoted yourself entirely to the welfare of the Depressed Classes, you would then become our hero.

G. Very sweet of you to say so.

A. I want political power for my community. That is indispensable for our survival. The basis of the agreement therefore should be: I should get what is due to me. I wish to tell the Hindus that I should be assured of my compensation.

G. You have clarified your position very beautifully. However, I should like to ask you one question. You say that if there is any genuine party among the Depressed Classes it should be given sufficient scope to rise. Therefore, their refusal to accept joint electorates without primary elections is quite reasonable. What I do not understand is why you have not said so far that there should be a separate election of this kind. I feel from whatever study I have made of the subject that if I accept the primary election, the letter of my vow is not violated. I, therefore, accept the Clause [of primary election] but I would most certainly have to scrutinize its wording. At the moment, I say only this, that the idea of separate primary elections does not go against my vow. But I suspect something when you insist that the panel should consist only of three candidates. It does not give me sufficient place to turn in.

Moreover, you consider panel system for some seats only, thereby satisfying both the parties [among *Harijans*]. There would be one election, i.e., of the primary nature by the Harijan voters only. The other would be by the joint electorate. I have to safeguard without any discrimination not the interest of one group alone but of the Depressed Class as a whole. I want to serve the untouchables. That is why I am not at all angry with you. When you use derogatory and angry words for me, I tell myself that I deserved that. I will not get angry even if you spit on my face. I say this with God as witness. I know that you have drunk deep of the poisoned cup. However, I make a claim which will seem astounding to you. You are born an untouchable but I am an untouchable by adoption. And as a new convert I feel more for the welfare of the community than those who are already there. At the moment I have before my eyes the dumb untouchables—unapproachables and unseeables—of South India. I am scrutinizing the scheme to see how these people will be affected by it. You will of course say why I should worry about that. All of you will either accept Christianity or Islam. I say that you may do whatever you like after my body falls. What I say is that if the panel system is good for the Depressed Classes it should be good for the entire electorate. I do not like it from the beginning that the community should be divided into two groups. I will raze to the ground the fort of sanatanists with dynamite if all the untouchables are one and united. I want that the entire untouchable community should unitedly rebel against the sanatanists. You should not worry about the number as long as the appointing power is in your hands. I am a lifelong democrat. The whole world will agree that I was the foremost among the democrats after my ashes are scattered in the air or, if that does not happen, after they are immersed in the Ganga. I do not say this out of pride but tell the truth with humility. I learnt the lesson of democracy at the tender age of 12. I quarrelled with my mother for treating the domestic sweeper as an untouchable. That day I saw God in the form of a *Bhangi.* You spoke the truth when you said that the welfare of untouchables is dearer to you than my own life. Now be honest and stick to it. You should not care for my life. But do not be false to *Harijans.* My work will not die with me. I have asked my son to convey my message to the Conference. In that, I have said that they should not be tempted to for the sake of the interests of the *Harijans* in order to save my life. I am sure that if I die my son will definitely follow me. Not only he but many others also will lay down their lives, for I do not have only one son, I have thousands. He would not be my worthy son if he did not lay down his life for the honour of Hinduism. Without eradicating untouchability root and branch the honour of Hinduism cannot be saved.

That can only happen when untouchables are treated on par with caste Hindus in every respect. A person who is regarded as 'unseeable' today should also have the opportunity to become the Viceroy of India. I had said, in the first political speech I made on coming to India that I would like to make a *Bhangi* the President of the Congress.

So I appeal to you not to haggle. Do not bring to me something which is so bad that I would not even like the look of it. Bring to me some nice present which would inspire life into a person who is willingly courting death. However, you will do that only if you are convinced that my co-operation has some value.

Appendix-2

Discussion with B.R. Ambedkar

October 17, 1932

AMBEDKAR: I have not come to discuss untouchability but political matters.

GANDHIJI: That is true. I cannot talk about it with you; even if you do I shall not be able to express an opinion—my mind does not work in that direction.

A. I have come here for this. I want to request you to give up civil disobedience and to join the Round Table Conference. The point is that if you do not come, we shall get nothing in England and everything will be upset. People like Iqbal who are enemies of the country will come to the forefront. We have to work any sort of Constitution. Hence, though I am a small man, I request you to come.

G. If you elabroate your argument, I shall think over it. I suggest you go and write about it at length in the newspapers. I shall think over it.

A. It is not a thing that can be put down in writing. In it I shall have to say a lot that will hurt the Muslims and I cannot say that publicly. But I shall write anonymously or have someone write in a different way. Please have a look at it and, taking it to be mine, think over it.

G. It will be good if you write under your own name. But of course you may do as you wish.

A. I must honestly say that I have no interest in the temples being thrown open, common dinners and the like, becuase we suffer thereby. My people have to put up with beatings and bitterness increases. After the common dinner at Vile Parle, the

Maratha workers went on strike. If the caste Hindus had the strength they would have engaged untouchables as servants. But that has not been so. Hence, I do not feel interested in the thing. I only want that social and economic hardships should end.

G. Give examples.

A. The untouchables do not get houses to live in; they continue to suffer injustice and oppression. In one case, an untouchable was accused of having murdered a Maratha. I could have taken the case to Sessions and got him acquitted, but the magistrate changed the charge of murder to one of grievous injury. Now he will receive some punishment. You may not know what even I have to face. I do not get any other place to live in Bombay except the Port Trust chawl. In my village, I have to stay in the midst of the Mahars. In Poona, all others stay with their friends. I have to stay at the National Hotel and have to spend Rs. 7 and transport fare.

G. Servants of India?

A. Yes, I can perhaps stay there. But only perhaps. You will know if you ask Vaze. Once Vaze's servant insulted me in his presence. I want to do away with all these hardships.

G. I am at one with you. You ought to know that my fast has not ended yet, it is still on. To correct the agreement was a minor thing. The main thing still remains to be done. I am ready to give my life for it. All the injustices you mention ought to end.

A. Birla said that I should be taken on the Committee for the Abolition of Untouchability. I declined to join, because what can I alone do? I would have to agree to the work of abolishing untouchability being done in accordance with your wishes.

If we are in a majority we can get the reforms that we wish

brought about. You wish that temples should be erected or wells should be dug. We might feel that that would be a waste of money, that there should be another way out for it.

G. I understand your point of view, and I shall keep it in mind and shall see what can be done.

Appendix-3

Statement on Fast to Anti-Untouchability Committee[2]

December 4, 1932

Although the Inspector-General gave me permission to say whatever I liked about the origin of the fast and what passed between Government and myself I do not want to take full advantage of the liberty he has given me. I shall only give you the substance of what happened so that you can be at ease and my position may not be misunderstood.

The fast which commenced yesterday, was, you will be glad to know, broken just before I came here. Mine is a peculiar position. Though I have hardened my heart there are things about which I have an exceedingly sensitive nature. To me there is no difference of degree in matters of moment and as I am capable of giving my life for a great cause I am equally capable of laying down my life for the life of a comrade.

Three Members of the Committee met him at 1 p.m. He was lying in bed and spoke in a low voice.

Now in the present case, the question before me was one of choice either to allow a dear comrade to die and myself live unconcerned or in an attempt to save his life put mine in jeopardy. Appasaheb Patwardhan, who is a prisoner in Ratnagiri Jail is an incorruptible man and a dear comrade whom I know to be cent per cent honest. I came to know through regular channels that Appasaheb had to put himself on the lowest diet consistent with bare existence for the service of untouchables which he wanted to do and which he was not permitted to do. I wrote to Government[1] in mildest language possible that if relief was not given to Appasaheb, I would have to go through the same agony and sacrifice as he was undergoing. He was and is going through slow death. I said I should have to fast. If I deserted him I would be capable of deserting the *Harijans*, and a man who deserts his comrades is not worth much. I had necessarily to give short notice because there was no choice for me.

Although I know that Appasaheb is a man of iron nerves, I could imagine what agonies a man on reduced rations would be going through and so I could not help giving short notice. I am glad to say that circumstances have arisen enabling me to break my fast though it does not mean that the chapter is closed. The Inspector-General of Prisons who was here is conferring with Government and pending Government's decision, which he hopes to get from Government on or before Wednesday morning, the fast stands suspended. But I have hopes I will not have to resume it. So far as my physical well-being is concerned I may say that I could not be better looked after than here and no one should run away with the idea that Government are not at all concerned about my life or they would like me to die in jail. They honestly want to see me discharged, if I am to be discharged at all, in full possession of health, that is to say, consistently with my age. In the present case I had asked for very little but perhaps Government thought it was too much; but I think they will now understand the delicate position and grant the relief which is sought for.[2] There are other matters also regarding the fast, but I do not like to go into them.

It will certainly be very good if the Government publishes the correspondence I had with it. But I leave it to the Government.

I hope what I told you is enough to give an assurance that I have not acted stupidly or hurriedly or unwisely. Knowing me as you do, you would wish me to act in the same manner should a similar occasion arise again. So far as I am concerned I should lose all my selfesteem and consider myself a despicable creature if I did not do all I was capable of doing in the contingency. For a man like me, who may not commit violence and who has taken a vow to observe non-violence in thought, word and deed, has self-sacrifice as a last resort. I depend on wisdom given by God to a small man like me and the weapon that I possess is readiness to fling away my life when there is a desperate cause. In this way my life is based on many such fasts. This is the highest form of prayer. The world has known it recently but I knew it for many years. It is not a thoughtless action. In it there is no coercion on others. It does bring pressure on individuals and the Government but is no more than the natural and moral outcome of self-sacrifice. It shakes and awakes the slumbering soul and impels a loving heart to action. The person, who has to introduce basic reforms in man, social conditions and atmosphere, has to create fermentation in the public. It cannot be brought about without causing a shake up in the society. There are only two ways of doing this—violence and non-violence. Violence affects the body and degrades both the person who commits it and the person who is the object of it. But in fasting the person suffers himself and the pressure brought about is of quite different kind. It does not affect the body of the person at whom it is directed but strengthens his morale or nature. I hope what I have told you is enough. Who knows I may have to go through a series of fasts and die by inches. But if that does happen I want you to feel proud of my action and not feel that it was the action of an imbecile. My life is largely governed by reason and, when it fails, it is governed by a superior force, that is, faith.

The Times of India, 5-12-1932

Notes

1. *Vide* "Letter to E.E. Doyle", 30-11-1932.
2. What follows has been translated from *Mahadevbhaini Diary*.

Appendix-4

Discussion with B.R. Ambedkar[1]

February 4, 1933

Discussing the propriety or otherwise of Ranga Iyer's two Bills [Ambedkar] said: The one-paragraph Bill is a very simple one. Its fair point lies in admitting that this custom is immoral. There is no such admission in the second Bill.

BAPU: No, it is there in its preamble.

Ambedkar. But it is not clear.... I also think that the two Bills do not go together...

BAPU: The one-paragraph Bill is certainly superior to the other. But the other lengthier Bill was brought forward because the first one could not be introduced in the Provincial Legislature. There is no contradiction in the two Bills. In one Bill untouchability ceases to be a disability and the law refuses to accept the argument based on untouchability. As a result of the second Bill, temple authorities are obliged to take steps under certain circumstances. If we can get both the Bills passed the trustees will not be able to put up any kind of obstacle. I take it upon myself to have all the temples opened within one month if we could get both the Bills passed. The sanatanists would prefer the second Bill. But speaking as a sincere sanatanist I would prefer the first Bill.

A.... Now the Government will have to issue orders against the sanatanists under Section 144 because they would be regarded as interfering with untouchables' rights.

BAPU: However, I want you now to emphatically proclaim your ideas in very clear words.

A.... As far as we are concerned we have no immediate concern other than securing political power... and that alone is the solution of our problem.... We want our social status raised in the eyes of the *Savarna* Hindus.

There is another point of view also. The object of this effort could be that you want the depressed classes to be retained in the Hindu religion, in which case I am inclined to believe that it is not sufficient in the present awakened state of the Depressed Classes.... If I call myself a Hindu I am obliged to accept that by birth I belong to a low caste. Hence, I think I must ask the Hindus to show me some sacred authority which would rule out this feeling of lowliness. If it cannot be I should say goodbye to Hinduism.... I am not going to be satisfied with measures which would merely bring some relief.... I don't want to be crushed by your charity.

BAPU: I have nothing to say if you have come with a final decision that you are not going to move your little finger to have this Bill passed.

A. We have not made any decision. However, I have shown you how my mind is working.

BAPU: I told you that I could have nothing to say if you have already taken a decision.

A. We cannot ask the *Savarna* Hindus to decide for themselves whether or not we are a part of them. You ought to demonstrate your determination by getting these Bills passed....

BAPU: I am not asking you to do anything. I never wanted the depressed people to go on their knees to the *Savarna* Hindus and ask them to get these Bills passed. Unfortunately, the solution of this problem is in the hands of a third power which is in a position to mend or worsen the situation.

A. I can set right the thing.

BAPU: That is right. Of course I agree with you that it does not behove your dignity to approach the Hindus. I take the position—you might remember since I made the speech at the Round Table Conference—that we should atone for this. If you repudiate us and go away I would think that we only deserved it.

A. The Bill mentions temple-entry but it makes no mention of entry into the sanctum sanctorum. Will they let a member of the depressed community place flowers on the idol, or will they let him offer a tray containing oblations? Malaviyaji has already declared that question of offering *puja* does not arise.

BAPU: Temple-entry is meant for *puja* if anything. But if the language of the Bill is not right it can be amended and we can say 'entry for the purpose of *puja*'. It seems there has been some misunderstanding somewhere in the case of Malaviyaji. He would not say what you attribute to him. Flowers, sweets or any other offerings from *Harijans* will surely be accepted. So we two agree on this point that there is no question of your imploring the *Savarna* Hindus. When some *Savarna* Hindus tell me that *Harijans* do not want to enter the temples I ask them to throw open the temple doors for the *Harijans* whether or not they wish to come in. They ought to have the satisfaction that they have done their duty. They ought to discharge the debt which they owe whether the creditor keeps it or throws it into the gutter. But I must say that you ought not to say that you are not a Hindu. In accepting the Poona Pact you accept the position that you are Hindus.

A. I have accepted only the political aspect of it.

BAPU: You cannot escape the situation that you are Hindus in spite of your statement to the contrary.

A. We ask of you that our silence should not be misconstrued. After that I accept your point.

BAPU: I go one step further. You will not be able to go ahead a single step unless you maintain your position absolutely correct. I regard temple-entry as a spiritual matter through which everything else will bear fruit.

A. The Hindu mind does not work in a rational way. They have no objection to the untouchables touching them on the railway and other public places. Why do they object to it only in the case of temples?

BAPU: We are well caught on this point. I take up the question of temple-entry first of all because these people want to cling to untouchability in the temples. Many sanatanist Hindus say that they would admit *Harijans* in schools and public places but not in temples. I ask them to grant the *Harijans* equal status before God. It will raise their status.

A. Supposing we are lucky in the case of temple-entry, will they let us fetch water from the wells?

BAPU: Sure. This is bound to follow it. And it is also very easy.

Note

1. *Vide* "Dr. Ambedkar and Caste", 7-2-1933.

Appendix-5

B.R. Ambedkar's Statement[1]

Although the controversy regarding the question of temple-entry is confined to the sanatanists and Mahatma Gandhi, the Depressed Classes have undoubtedly a very important part to play in it, in so far as their position is bound to weigh the scale one way or the other, when the issue comes for a final settlement. It is, therefore, necessary that their viewpoint should be defined and stated so as to leave no ambiguity about it.

To the Temple-entry Bill of Mr. Ranga Iyer as now drafted, the Depressed Classes cannot possibly give their support. The principle of the Bill is that if a majority of municipal and local board voters in the vicinity of any particular temple on a referendum decide by a majority that the Depressed Classes shall be allowed to enter the temple, the trustees or the manager of the temple shall give effect to that decision. The principle is an ordinary principle of majority rule, and there is nothing radical or revolutionary about the Bill, and if the sanatanists were a wise lot they would accept it without demur.

The reasons why the Depressed Classes cannot support a Bill based upon this principle are two. One reason is that the Bill cannot hasten the day of temple-entry for the Depressed Classes any nearer than otherwise would be the case. It is true that under the Bill, the minority will not have the right to obtain an injunction against the trustee, or the manager who throws open the temple to the Depressed Classes in accordance with the decision of the majority. But before one can draw any satisfaction from this clause and congratulate the author of the Bill, one must first of all feel assured that when the question is put to the vote, there will be a majority in favour of temple-entry. If one is not suffering from illusions of any kind, one must accept that the hope of a majority voting in favour of temple-entry will be very rarely realized if at all. Without doubt, the majority is definitely opposed today—a fact which is conceded by the author of the Bill himself in his correspondence with the Shankaracharya.

What is there in the situation as created after the passing of the Bill, which can lead one to hope that the majority will act differently? I find nothing. I shall, no doubt, be reminded of the results of the referendum with regard to the Guruvayur Temple. But I refuse to accept a referendum, so overweighted as it was by the life of Mahatma Gandhi, as the normal result. In any such calculations, the life of the Mahatma must necessarily be deducted.

If Hindu religion is to be a religion of social equality, then an amendment of its code to provide temple-entry is not enough. What is required is to purge it of the doctrine of *Chaturvarnya*.

The Bombay Chronicle, 13-2-1933

Note

1. *Vide* "Interview to Associated Press", 14-2-1933 and "Letter to C. Rajagopalachari", 22-2-1933

Appendix-6

Dr. Ambedkar's Indictment-I

The readers will recall the fact that Dr. Ambedkar was to have presided last May at the annual conference of the Jat-Pat-Torak Mandal of Lahore. But the conference itself was cancelled because Dr. Ambedkar's address was found by the Reception Committee to be unacceptable. How far a Reception Committee is justified in rejecting a President of its choice because of his address that may be objectionable to it is open to question. The Committee knew Dr. Ambedkar's views on caste and the Hindu scriptures. They knew also that he had in unequivocal terms decided to give up Hinduism. Nothing less than the address that Dr. Ambedkar had prepared was to be expected from him. The Committee appears to have deprived the public of an opportunity of listening to the original views of a man who has carved out for himself a unique position in society. Whatever label he wears in future, Dr. Ambedkar is not the man to allow himself to be forgotten.

Dr. Ambedkar was not going to be beaten by the Reception Committee. He has answered their rejection of him by publishing the address at his own expense. He has priced it at 8 annas. I would suggest a reduction to 2 annas or at least 4 annas.

No reformer can ignore the address. The orthodox will gain by reading it. This is not to say that the address is not open to objection.

It has to be read if only because it is open to serious objection. Dr. Ambedkar is a challenge to Hinduism. Brought up as a Hindu, educated by a Hindu potentiate, he has become so disgusted with the so-called *Savarna* Hindus for the treatment that he and his have received at their hands that he proposes to leave not only them but the very religion that is his and their common heritage. He has transferred to that religion his disgust against a part of its professors.

But this is not to be wondered at. After all one can only judge a system or an institution by the conduct of its representatives. What is more, Dr. Ambedkar found that the vast majority of *Savarna* Hindus had not only conducted themselves inhumanly against those of their fellow religionists whom they classed as untouchables, but they had based their conduct on the authority of their scriptures, and when he began to search them he had found ample warrant for their belief in untouchability and all its implications. The author of the address has quoted chapter and verse in proof of his therefold indictment—inhuman conduct itself, the unabashed justification for it on the part of the prepetrators, and the subsequent discovery that the justification was warranted by their scriptures.

No Hindu who prizes his faith above life itself can afford to underrate the importance of this indictment. Dr. Ambedkar is not alone in his disgust. He is its most uncompromising exponent and one of the ablest among them. He is certainly the most irreconcilable among them. Thank God, in the front rank of the leaders he is singularly alone and as yet but a representative of a very small minority.

But what he says is voiced with more or less vehemence by many leaders belonging to the Depressed Classes. Only the latter, for instance Rao Bahadur M.C. Rajah and Dewan Bahadur Srinivasan, not only do not threaten to give up Hinduism but find enough warmth in it to compensate for the shameful persecution to which the vast mass of *Harijans* are exposed.

But the fact of many leaders remaining in the Hindu fold is no warrant for disregarding what Dr. Ambedkar has to say. The *Savarnas* have to correct their belief and their conduct. Above all, those who are by their learning and influence among the *Savarnas* have to give an authoritative interpretaion of the scriptures. The questions that Dr. Ambedkar's indictment suggests are:

1. What are the scriptures?
2. Are all the printed texts to be regarded as an integral part of them or is any part of them to be rejected as unauthorized interpolations?
3. What is the answer of such accepted and expurgated scriptures on the question of untouchability, caste, equality of status, inter-dining and intermarriages? (These have been all ably examined by Dr. Ambedkar in his address).

I must reserve for the next issue[1] my own answer to these questions and a statement of the (at least some) manifest flaws in Dr. Ambedkar's thesis.

—*Harijan*, 11-7-1936

Note

1. *Vide* "Dr. Ambedkar's Indictment—11", 18-7-1936.

Appendix-7

Dr. Ambedkar's Indictment-II

The Vedas, Upanishads, *Smritis* and *Puranas* including *Ramayana* and *Mahabharata* are the Hindu scriptures. Nor is this a finite list. Evey age or even generation has added to the list. It follows, therefore, that everything printed or even found handwritten is not scripture. The *Smritis*, for instance, contain much that can never be accepted as the word of God. Thus many of the texts that Dr. Ambedkar quotes from the *Smritis* cannot be accepted as authentic. The scriptures properly so called can only be concerned with eternal verities and must appeal to any conscience, i.e., any heart whose eyes of understanding are opened. Nothing can be accepted as the word of God which cannot be tested by reason or is not capable of being spiritually experienced. And even when you have an expurgated edition of the scriptures, you will need their interpretation. Who is the best interpreter? Not learned men surely. Learning there must be. But religion does not live by it. It lives in the experiences of its saints and seers, in their lives and sayings. When all the most learned commentators of the scriptures are utterly forgotten, the accumulated experience of the sages and saints will abide and be an inspiration for ages to come.

Caste has nothing to do with religion. It is a custom whose origin I do not know and do not need to know for the satisfaction of my spiritual hunger. But I do know, that it is harmful both to spiritual and national growth. *Varnas* and *ashramas* are institutions which have nothing to do with castes. The law of *varna* teaches us that we have each one of us to earn our bread by following the ancestral calling. It defines not our rights but our duties. It necessarily has reference to callings that are conducive to the welfare of humanity and to no other.

It also follows that there is no calling too low and none too high. All are good, lawful, and absolutely equal in status. The callings of a Brahmin—spiritual teacher—and a scavenger are equal, and their due performance carries equal merit before God and at one time seems to have carried identical reward before man. Both were entitled to their livelihood and no more. Indeed one traces even now in the villages the faint lines of this healthy operation of the law. Living in Segaon with its population of 600, I do not find a great disparity between the earnings of different tradesmen including Brahmins. I find too that real Brahmins are to be found even in these degenerate days who are living on alms freely given to them and are giving freely of what they have of spiritual treasures. It would be wrong and improper to judge the law of varna by its caricature in the lives of men who profess to belong to a varna whilst they openly commit a breach of its only operative rule. Arrogation of a superior status by any of the *varnas* over another is a denial of the law. And there is nothing in the law of varna to warrant a belief in untouchability. (The essence of Hinduism is contained in its enunciation of one and only God as Truth and its bold acceptance of *ahimsa* as the law of the human family.)

I am aware that my interpretation of Hinduism will be disputed by many besides Dr. Ambedkar. That does not affect my position. It is an interpretation by which I have lived for nearly half a century and according to which I have endeavoured to the best of my ability to regulate my life.

In my opinion the profound mistake that Dr. Ambedkar has made in his address is to pick out the texts of doubtful authenticity and value and the state of degraded Hindus who are no fit specimens of the faith they, so woefully misrepresent. Judged by the standard applied by Dr. Ambedkar, every known living faith will probably fail.

In his able address, the learned Doctor has over-proved his case. Can a religion that was professed by Chaitanya, Jnanadeva, Tukaram, Tiruvalluvar, Ramakrishna Paramahamsa, Raja Ram Mohan Roy, Maharshi Devendranath Tagore, Vivekananda and a host of others who might be easily mentioned, be so utterly devoid of merit as is made out in Dr. Ambedkar's address? A religion has to be judged not by its worst specimens but by the best it might have produced. For that and that alone can be used as the standard to aspire to, if not to improve upon.

Harijan, 18-7-1936

Index